BIRDS of Seattle and Puget Sound

Chris C. Fisher

First printed in 1996 10 9 8 7 6

Printed in Canada

The Publisher: Lone Pine Publishing

1901 Raymond Ave. SW, Suite C	202A, 1110 Seymour St.	206, 10426 – 81 Ave.
Renton, Washington	Vancouver, British Columbia	Edmonton, Alberta
U.S.A. 98055	Canada V6B 3N3	Canada T6E 1X5

Canadian Cataloguing in Publication Data

Fisher, Chris C. (Christopher Charles)
Birds of Seattle and Puget Sound

Includes bibliographical references and index.
ISBN 1-55105-078-1

1. Birds—Washington (State)—Seattle—Identification. 2. Birds—Washington (State)—Puget Sound Region—Identification. 3. Bird watching—Washington (State)—Seattle. 4. Bird watching—Washington (State)—Puget Sound Region. I. Title.
QL684.W2F57 1996 598.29797'7 C96-910609-2

Senior Editor: Nancy Foulds
Editorial: Jennifer Keane, Roland Lines
Design and Layout: Carol S. Dragich
Cover Design: Carol S. Dragich
Cover Illustration: Gary Ross
Technical Review: Dennis Paulson, Wayne Campbell, Kevin Aanerud
Separations and Film: Elite Lithographers Co. Ltd., Edmonton, Alberta, Canada
Printing: Quality Color Press Inc., Edmonton, Alberta, Canada

The publisher gratefully acknowledges the support of Alberta Community Development and the Department of Canadian Heritage.

All illustrations are by **Gary Ross**, except as follows:

Ewa Pluciennik: 3 (bottom right), 8, 12 (second from top), 18, 20, 25, 40, 44, 46, 69, 76, 79, 85, 99, 102, 110, 126, 134, 140, 160.
Ted Nordhagen: 15 (third from top), 135, 136, 142.
Horst Krause: 27, 148.

Contents

Acknowledgments

A book such as this is made possible by the inspired work of Seattle's naturalist community. Their contributions continue to advance the science of ornithology and to motivate a new generation of nature lovers.

My thanks to Gary Ross, Ewa Pluciennik, Ted Nordhagen and Horst Krause, whose illustrations have elevated the quality of this book; Carole Patterson for her continual support; Mary Dzieweczynski for her useful suggestions and kindness; Wayne Campbell, Eugene Hunn, Dennis Paulson and Terence Wahl, premier naturalists whose works have served as models of excellence; the active Seattle Audubon Society, which makes daily contributions to natural history, and is clearly one of the finest of such organizations in America; the team at Lone Pine Publishing—Shane Kennedy, Jennifer Keane, Carol Dragich, Nancy Foulds and Roland Lines—for their input and steering; and John Acorn and Jim Butler for their stewardship and their remarkable passion. Finally, my thanks go to Dennis Paulson, Wayne Campbell and Kevin Aanerud for their thorough and helpful review of the text.

Introduction

No matter where we live, birds are a natural part of our lives. We are so used to seeing them that we often take their presence for granted. When we take the time to notice their colors, songs and behaviors, we experience their dynamic appeal.

This book presents a brief introduction to the lives of birds. It is intended to serve as a bird identification and appreciation guide. Getting to know the names of birds is the first step towards getting to know birds. Once we've made contact with a species, we can better appreciate its character and mannerisms during future encounters. Over a lifetime of meetings, many birds become acquaintances, some seen daily, others not for years.

The selection of species in this book represents a balance between the familiar and the noteworthy. Many of the 125 species described here are the most common species found in Seattle. Some are less common, but they are noteworthy because they are important ecologically or because their particular status grants them a high profile. It would be impossible for a beginners' book such as this to comprehensively describe all the birds found in the Seattle area. Furthermore, there is no one site where all the species described in this book can be observed simultaneously. Most species, however, can be viewed—at least seasonally—in or near Seattle. Washington State is blessed with three excellent bird-finding guides (Hunn 1982, MacRae 1995, Wahl and Paulson 1991) to help birders looking for a specific species.

It is hoped that this guide will inspire novice birdwatchers into spending some time outdoors, gaining valuable experience with the local bird community. This book stresses identifying birds, but it also attempts to bring them to life by discussing their various character traits. We often discuss a bird's character in human terms to help us feel a bond with the bird, but these personifications should not be mistaken as representing actual interpretations of bird behavior. Birds' lives and behaviors are very complex, and our interpretations can falsely suggest a lack of complexity.

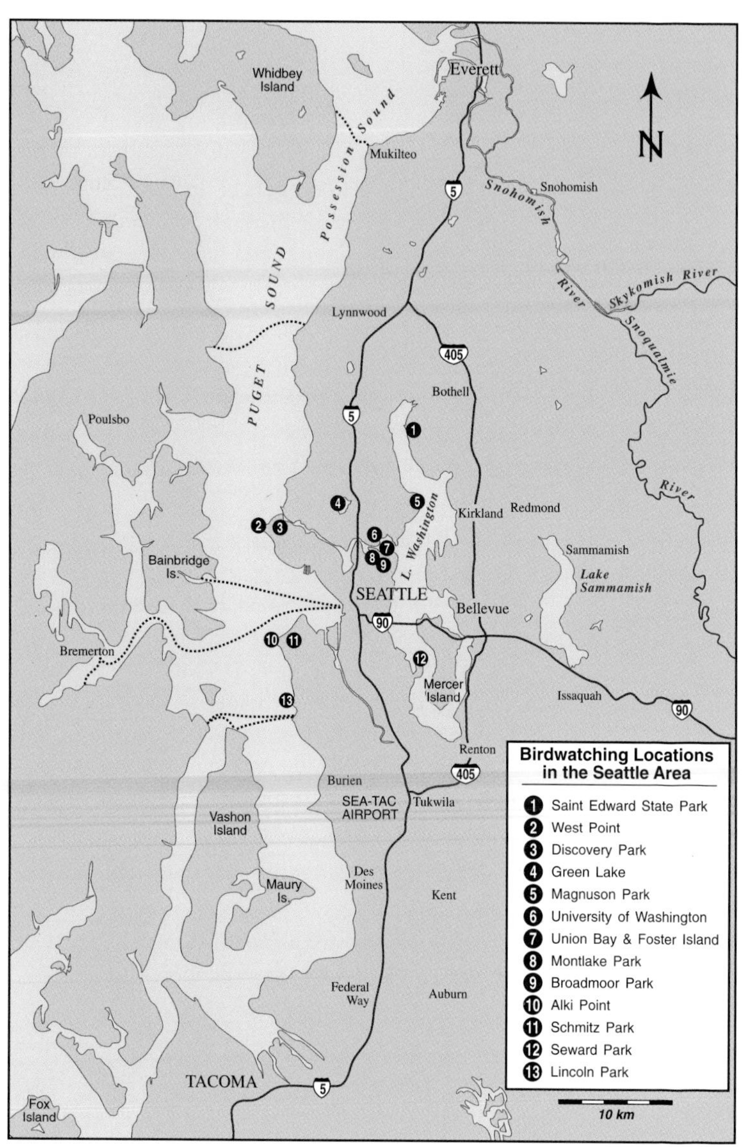

Whidbey Island
Everett
Possession Sound
Mukilteo
Snohomish
Snohomish River
Skykomish River
Snoqualmie River
PUGET SOUND
Lynnwood
Bothell
Poulsbo
Kirkland
Redmond
L. Washington
Sammamish
Lake Sammamish
Bainbridge Is.
SEATTLE
Bellevue
Bremerton
Mercer Island
Issaquah
Renton
Burien
SEA-TAC AIRPORT
Tukwila
Vashon Island
Maury Is.
Des Moines
Kent
Federal Way
Auburn
TACOMA
Fox Island
N
10 km
Birdwatching Locations in the Seattle Area
1 Saint Edward State Park
2 West Point
3 Discovery Park
4 Green Lake
5 Magnuson Park
6 University of Washington
7 Union Bay & Foster Island
8 Montlake Park
9 Broadmoor Park
10 Alki Point
11 Schmitz Park
12 Seward Park
13 Lincoln Park

FEATURES OF THE LANDSCAPE

Seattle lies within a major bird migration route known as the Pacific Flyway. Along this corridor, birds move north in the spring and south in the fall, following geologic features, such as shorelines and mountains. Along the shorelines, sandpipers, geese and many other waterbirds move from one productive foraging site to another. Many land birds follow the eastern edge of the Cascades in their migration; the coastal mountain ranges also guide birds in their north-south travel.

Seattle's bird life is not restricted to peak migratory periods: our region is blessed with a year-round diversity. Relatively mild winters and pleasant summers support a wide variety of birds, and all seasons have their specialties.

The open waters of Puget Sound are a blessing to the Seattle birdwatching community. Whether you scan the waters from a viewpoint or from a boat, the Sound reliably hosts loons, grebes, alcids and cormorants. The shorelines of Seattle can be viewed from many of the same vantage points. Expect cormorants, gulls and ducks in rocky areas, while sandy beaches and exposed tidal flats may host gulls, terns, waterfowl and the occasional shorebird.

Within the city of Seattle there are pockets of bird life. Lush parks and gardens attract many songbirds that commonly bred in the area before extensive urbanization. The landscaped settings are some of the best places to become familiar with Seattle's bird life; the birds you will find there often accept human company. Backyard feeders and nest boxes invite many species of songbirds to enter into mutually beneficial relationships with their human neighbors. Even within the city's most modified areas you will find birds—those that are well adapted to urban areas, such as pigeons, sparrows and starlings.

Freshwater lakes attract seasonal concentrations of waterbirds. Wintering birds feed on the abundant animal and plant life, and during the breeding season many birds nest along the shorelines. Although the larger freshwater lakes may superficially resemble the saltwater Puget Sound, many birds discriminate between the two habitats.

One of the most uncommon yet most productive habitats is the marsh. These wet areas are bonanzas for bird life. Unfortunately, Seattle's salt marshes were drained long ago, and the remaining freshwater marshes are continually being destroyed by urban sprawl. Some nice examples of marsh still remain along the edges of Lake Washington at Juanita Bay and Union Bay.

Fields and meadows are also uncommon around Seattle, and they are generally confined to agricultural areas. Despite this narrow distribution, raptors, meadowlarks and blackbirds can reliably be seen in the region's open areas.

Moist coniferous forests—mainly Douglas-fir, western hemlock and red cedar—dominate the landscape around Seattle. Winter Wrens, warblers and other songsters are the most common birds. Broadleaf forests are also abundant in the Seattle area. They tend to be drier than coniferous woods, but they can be equally diverse. The limbs of red alder, Pacific madrone and maple trees frequently host chickadees, vireos and Band-tailed Pigeons.

Many bird species in and around Seattle are able to inhabit a variety of lowland habitats. Outside Seattle, the forest community changes with altitude and the bird community changes considerably above 3000 feet. Many species are found exclusively in these high altitudes. Several species occur in greater numbers in coniferous forests high above the lowlands than they do elsewhere. The voices of Western Tanagers and Townsend's Warblers grace the canopies, and the hooting of Blue Grouse and the rare Spotted Owl can still be heard.

THE IMPORTANCE OF HABITAT

Understanding the relationship between habitat and bird species often helps in identifying birds. Because you won't find a loon up a tree or a grouse out at sea, habitat is an important factor to consider when birdwatching.

The quality of habitat is one of the most powerful factors to influence bird distribution, and with experience you may become amazed by the predictability of some birds within a specific habitat type.

Habitat Icons

Each bird description in this guide is includes at least one habitat icon to represent the general habitat or habitats in which the bird is most likely to be seen. These habitat categories will work in most situations, but migrants can turn up in just about any habitat type. These unexpected surprises can confuse novice birders, but they are among the most powerful motivations for the increasing legion of birdwatchers.

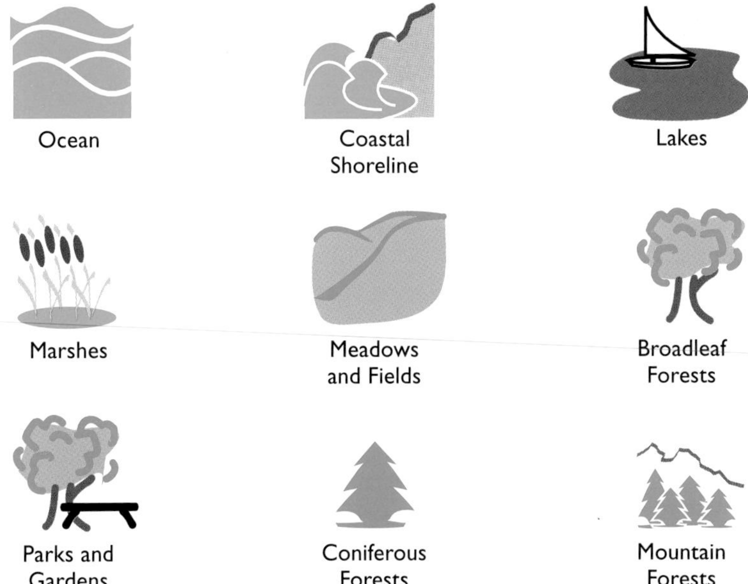

THE ORGANIZATION OF THIS BOOK

To simplify field identification, this book is organized slightly differently from the many other field guides that use strict phylogenetic order. In cases where many birds from the same family are described, conventional groupings are maintained. In other cases, however, distantly related birds that share physical and behavioral similarities are grouped together. This blend of grouping by family and by physical similarities is structured to help the novice birdwatcher identify the birds he or she encounters.

DIVING BIRDS

loons, grebes, cormorants

These heavy-bodied birds are adapted to diving for their food. Between underwater foraging dives, they are most frequently seen on the water's surface. These birds could be confused only with one another or with certain diving ducks.

WETLAND WADERS

herons, rails, coots

Although this group varies considerably in size and represents two separate families of related birds, wetland waders share similar habitat and food preferences. Some of these long-legged birds of marshes are quite common, but certain species are heard far more often than they are seen.

WATERFOWL

swans, geese, ducks

Waterfowl tend to have stout bodies and webbed feet, and they are swift in flight. Most species are associated with water, but some can occasionally be seen grazing on upland sites.

HAWKS AND EAGLES

From deep forests to open country to large lakes, there are hawks and eagles hunting the skies. Their predatory look—with sharp talons, hooked bills and forward-facing eyes—easily identifies this group. Hawks and eagles generally forage during the day, and many use their broad wings to soar in thermals and updrafts.

GAMEBIRDS

pheasants, grouse, quail
These birds bear a superficial resemblance to chickens. They are stout birds and poor fliers, and they are most often encountered on the ground or when they are flushed.

SHOREBIRDS

plovers, sandpipers, etc.
Shorebirds are usually confined to the shores and tidal flats of the ocean and larger lakes. Although these small, long-legged, swift-flying birds are mainly found on our shorelines, don't be surprised to find some species in pastures and marshy areas.

GULLS AND TERNS

Gulls are relatively large, light-colored birds that are frequently seen in the Seattle area as they swim, walk around urban areas or soar gracefully over the city. Their backs tend to be darker than their bellies, and their feet are webbed. Terns are in the same family as gulls, but they are smaller and they are much less likely to be seen on the ground.

ALCIDS

murres, guillemots, auklets

These stocky, stubby-winged birds are found exclusively on the ocean or nesting on steep or isolated outcrops. They are relatively small and compact, and they swim underwater using their short, firm wings. They are poor fliers, and they need to beat their small wings quickly to stay airborne. 'Alcid' is a term used to denote the auk family, to which these birds belong.

PIGEONS

Both of Seattle's pigeon species are easily recognizable. Rock Doves are found in all urban areas, from city parks to the downtown core. The less-urbanized Band-tailed Pigeon has many of the same physical and behavioral characteristics as its urban kin.

OWLS

These night hunters have forward-facing eyes, a facial disk and a large, rounded head, and they are armed with powerful talons and a strongly hooked bill. Although owls are primarily active at night, their distinctive calls enable birdwatchers to readily identify these birds.

HUMMINGBIRDS

Hummingbirds are Seattle's smallest birds; they are brightly colored and are swift fliers.

KINGFISHERS

Kingfishers plunge after fish from the air or from an overhanging perch. Their behavior and physical characteristics are unlike those of any bird in Seattle.

WOODPECKERS

The drumming sound of hammering wood and their precarious foraging habits easily identify most woodpeckers. They are frequently seen in forests, clinging to trunks and chipping away bark with their straight, sturdy bills. Even when these birds cannot be seen or heard, the characteristic marks of certain species can be seen on trees in any mature forest.

FLYCATCHERS

This family is best identified by its foraging behavior: flycatchers catch insects by darting after them from a favorite perch. Most flycatchers sing simple but distinctive songs, which help to identify them far more effectively than their subdued plumage.

SWIFTS AND SWALLOWS

Members of these two families are typically seen at their nest site or in flight. Small but sleek, swallows fly gracefully and catch insects in mid-air. Although swallows are superficially similar to swifts in behavior and appearance, the two groups are not closely related. Swifts are small, dark birds with long narrow wings and a short tail. They are nearly always seen in flight.

JAYS AND CROWS

Members of this family are familiar to many people. Intelligent and adaptable, these easily observed birds are often extremely bold. They are sometimes called 'corvids,' from Corvidae, the scientific name for the family.

SMALL SONGBIRDS

chickadees, nuthatches, wrens, kinglets, etc.

Birds in this group are all generally smaller than a sparrow. Many of them associate with one another in mixed-species flocks. Most are year-round residents and, with the exception of the Marsh Wren, they are commonly encountered in city parks and backyards.

THRUSHES

From the robin to the secretive forest thrushes, this group of beautiful singers has the finest collective voice. Although some thrushes are very familiar, sighting others requires a little experience and patience.

WARBLERS AND VIREOS

Warblers and vireos are very diverse in plumage: warblers tend to be liberally splashed with colors, while vireos dress in pale olive. These birds are all very small and sing characteristic courtship songs.

MID-SIZED SONGBIRDS

tanagers, starlings, waxwings

The birds in this group are all sized between a sparrow and a robin. Tanagers are very colorful and sing complex, flute-like songs, while the tan-coloured waxwings are more reserved in dress and voice. Starlings are frequently seen and heard all around Seattle.

SPARROWS

towhees, sparrows, juncos

These small, often nondescript birds are predominantly brown. Their songs are often very useful in identification. Some birdwatchers discount many sparrows as simply 'little brown birds'; this is unfortunate, since these birds are worthy of the extra effort to identify. The towhee is a colorful member of the sparrow clan.

BLACKBIRDS

blackbirds, meadowlarks, cowbirds, orioles

These birds are predominantly black and have relatively long tails. They are common in open areas, city parks and agricultural fields.

FINCHES

finches, grosbeaks, etc.

Finches are year-round residents in Seattle. They are primarily adapted to feeding on seeds, and they have stout, conical bills. Many are birdfeeder regulars, and they are a familiar part of the Seattle winter scene. The finch-like, ubiquitous, introduced House Sparrow is also included in this group. It resembles our native sparrows, but it has shorter legs and a thicker beak.

Abundance Charts

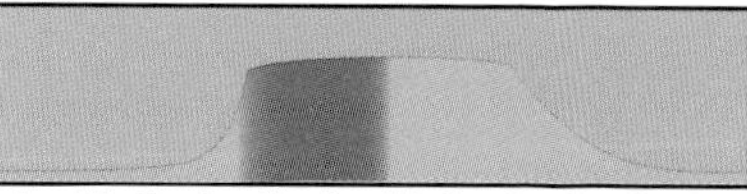

Accompanying each bird description is a chart that indicates the relative abundance of the species through the year. These stylized graphs offer some insight into the distribution and abundance of the birds, but they represent a generalized overview and should not be viewed as definitive. There will be inconsistencies specific to time and location, but these charts should provide readers with a basic reference for bird abundance and occurrence.

Each chart is divided into the twelve months of the year. The pale orange that colors the chart is an indication of abundance—the more color, the more common the bird. The dark orange color is used to indicate the nesting period. As there is little information on breeding dates, the time frame is approximate, and nesting birds can be found both before and after the period indicated on the chart. Where no nesting color is shown, the bird breeds outside Seattle area—most often to the north and east—and visit Seattle in significant numbers during migration or during winter.

These graphs are based on personal observations and on Eugene Hunn's *Birding in Seattle and King County* (1982).

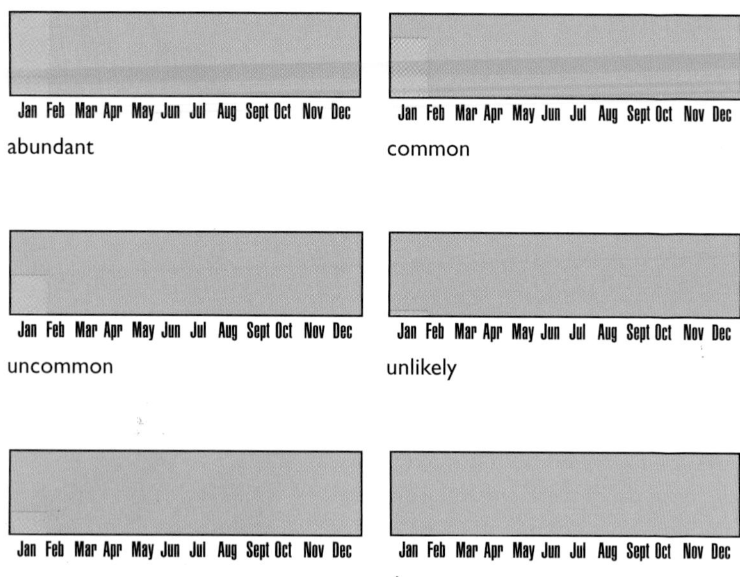

BIRDS of Seattle and Puget Sound

Common Loon

Gavia immer

Jan Feb Mar Apr May Jun Jul Aug Sept Oct Nov Dec

Quick I.D.: goose-sized.
Non-breeding: mottled gray-brown above, white below; light band partway across mid-neck; bill stout and sharp; hunchbacked in flight; sexes similar.
Size: 30–34 in.

Loons are highly adapted and therefore restricted to their aquatic lifestyle. Because they have solid, heavy bones (unlike chickens and most other birds, which have hollow bones) and because their legs are placed well back on their bodies for diving, Common Loons require long stretches of open water for takeoff.

Their intricate dark green (almost black) and white breeding wardrobe gives way to winter browns as hundreds of these birds quietly spend the winter months on Puget Sound. Nature lovers can observe loons in the rolling waves at Alki Point or West Point.

Similar Species: Red-throated Loon and Pacific Loon have slimmer bills and lack the light band across the mid-neck; Yellow-billed Loon has 'browner' plumage and its bill angles slightly upwards; cormorants (pp. 23–24) are generally darker and have longer necks; alcids (pp. 72–75) are much smaller.

Pied-billed Grebe

Podilymbus podiceps

The small, stout, drab body of the Pied-billed Grebe seems perfectly suited to its marshy habitat, but its loud, whooping *kuk-kuk-cow-cow-cow-cowp-cowp* is a sound that seems more at home in tropical rainforests.

Pied-billed Grebes can be found on most freshwater wetlands that are surrounded by emergent vegetation, such as cattails and bulrushes. Montlake Fill and Green Lake usually produce several of these small, reclusive grebes. Pied-billed Grebes are frustrating to follow as they appear and disappear from the still waters and water lilies of these urban wetlands.

Many Pied-billed Grebes remain in Seattle during the summer; they build their nests within view of lakeside trails. Grebes build nests that float on the water's surface, and their eggs often rest in waterlogged vegetation. After hatching, young grebes soon take their first swim, but they will instinctively clamber aboard a parent's back should any danger suddenly arise.

Similar Species: Ducks have bills that are flattened top to bottom; Horned Grebe (p. 22) and Eared Grebe have light underparts.

Quick I.D.: smaller than a duck; all-brown.
Breeding: dark vertical band on thick, pale bill; black chin; sexes similar.
First-year young (summer/fall): striped brown and white.
Size: 12–14 in.

Jan Feb Mar Apr May Jun Jul Aug Sept Oct Nov Dec

Horned Grebe

Podiceps auritus

Quick I.D.: smaller than a duck; white cheek; dark crown and upperparts; light underneath; bill shorter than width of the head; red eyes; sexes similar.
Size: 12½–15 in.

Like many waterbirds that winter in the Seattle area, Horned Grebes lose their splendid summer plumage and assume low-key black and white coloring. So dramatic is their transformation that, from their summer wardrobe (seen briefly in April before their departure), only their blood-red eyes remain. Horned Grebes are abundant in shallow, protected bays from September through April, and they are commonly seen on Puget Sound and Lake Washington. Their behavior is characteristically peppy: they leap up before diving neatly headfirst into the water.

All grebes eat feathers, a seemingly strange habit that frequently results in their digestive systems becoming packed. It is thought that this behavior may protect their stomachs from sharp fish bones, and it may also slow the passage of the bones through the digestive system so that more nutrients are absorbed. The toes of grebes are also unusual: unlike the fully webbed feet of ducks, gulls, cormorants and alcids, grebes' toes are individually lobed.

Similar Species: Non-breeding Red-necked Grebe (p. 22) is much larger, and has gray cheeks and a heavy bill; Eared Grebe is uncommon, is the same size, and has dark cheeks; Pied-billed Grebe (p. 19) has dark underparts and is almost always in freshwater.

Western Grebe

Aechmophorus occidentalis

Coastal residents are fortunate to have unsurpassed concentrations of this winter visitor. If you gaze out onto Puget Sound from Alki Point or West Point, or if you scan Lake Washington, you will frequently have brief, intermittent glimpses of these grebes riding the troughs and peaks of the waves.

The distinguished look of the Western Grebe is refined by its formal plumage, ruby eyes, cobra-like head, and long, stiletto bill. Unlike that of other overwintering grebes, the Western's plumage doesn't change over the seasons. The Western Grebe is easily identified by its long, graceful neck as it fishes the open waters for the small fish it pierces with its dagger-like bill.

Similar Species: Red-necked Grebe (p. 22) has a shorter gray neck and a thicker bill; Clark's Grebe (rare but regular in Seattle) lacks the black mask through the eye.

Quick I.D.: duck-sized; very long neck; black upperparts; yellow-green bill; black mask through eye; white underparts; long bill; sexes similar.
Size: 23–28 in.

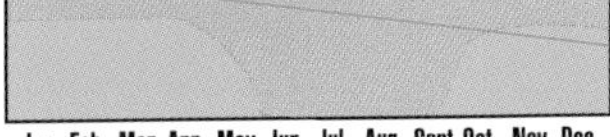

Jan Feb Mar Apr May Jun Jul Aug Sept Oct Nov Dec

Red-necked Grebe

Podiceps grisegena

Quick I.D.: duck-sized; medium-length neck; straight bill; dark eyes; very short tail; sexes similar.
Breeding: red neck; white cheek.
Non-breeding: white crescent on face; gray cheek; dusky throat; black cap; light upperparts; gray flanks and neck.
Size: 18–20½ in.

Jan Feb Mar Apr May Jun Jul Aug Sept Oct Nov Dec

The Red-necked Grebe, which is mainly seen from mid-October to the end of February, retreats to the protected waters off Seattle during the winter and spends the cold months in solitude. Sometimes this stocky grebe may be seen with loose flocks of scoters, goldeneyes and other waterbirds, but most Red-necked Grebes are observed singly or in small groups.

The Red-necked Grebe dives below the water's surface for sculpins, Pacific herring, minnows, shrimp and other aquatic animals. The foraging dives are generally short journeys, and the bird is often seen rising to the surface nearby less than a minute after it initially disappeared. During the winter this grebe loses most of the red color in its neck; its species name *grisegena* (Latin for 'gray cheek') celebrates this bird's darker winter plumage.

Similar Species: Horned Grebe (p. 20) has a dark cheek and a shorter neck; Eared Grebe has a dark neck; Pied-billed Grebe (p. 19) has a thicker bill, and its body is mostly brown; Western Grebe (p. 21) has black upperparts, white underparts and a long neck that is white in front and dark in back.

Double-crested Cormorant

Phalacrocorax auritus

The Double-crested Cormorant is a common sight on the West Coast, and it is the only cormorant that ventures inland. Like Pelagic and Brandt's cormorants, Double-crests fly in single-file, low over Puget Sound. At Green Lake and inland lakes, however, only Double-crests are seen.

Cormorants lack the ability to waterproof their wings, so they need to dry their wings after each swim. These large black waterbirds are frequently seen perched on seawalls, bridge pilings and buoys, with their wings partially spread to expose their wet feathers to the sun and wind. It would seem to be a great disadvantage for a waterbird to have to dry its wings, but the cormorant's ability to wet its feathers decreases its buoyancy, making it easier for it to swim after the fish on which it preys. Sealed nostrils, a long, rudder-like tail and excellent underwater vision are other features of the Double-crested Cormorant's aquatic lifestyle.

Similar Species: Pelagic Cormorant (p. 24) flies with a straight neck, is dark green and iridescent in bright light, has white saddle patches and has a red throat pouch in breeding plumage; Brandt's Cormorant is slightly larger, flies with its neck outstretched, and has a relatively short tail; non-breeding loons and large, dark ducks and geese generally have shorter necks and are more stout over-all.

Quick I.D.: goose-sized; large, black waterbird; long tail; long neck; sexes similar.
Flight: kinked neck; rapid wingbeats.
Breeding: bright orange throat pouch; white plumes streaming back from eyebrows (seen only at close range).
Immature: brown; pale neck, breast and belly.
Size: 30–35 in.

Jan Feb Mar Apr May Jun Jul Aug Sept Oct Nov Dec

Pelagic Cormorant

Phalacrocorax pelagicus

The Pelagic Cormorant is all black, and it is the smallest and slimmest cormorant of the West Coast. Like the closely related pelicans, cormorants have a naked throat pouch and fully webbed feet (all four toes are linked with webbing). Cormorants overheat easily, and they are frequently seen during hot weather with their bills open, panting to cool off. Cormorant colonies are sensitive to human disturbances, and they are not found very near to Seattle. Pelagic Cormorants nest precariously on thin cliff ledges, laying their eggs in meager nests of seaweed and guano.

In Seattle, the Pelagic Cormorant can best be observed on Puget Sound from Alki Point or West Point. Double-crested Cormorants are also common; to identify the Pelagic, look for the cormorants that hold their neck straight out in flight and sport two white saddle patches during the breeding season (late winter to early summer).

Similar Species: Double-crested Cormorant (p. 23) is larger and its neck is kinked in flight; Brandt's Cormorant is larger, flies with its neck outstretched, and has a relatively short tail; non-breeding loons and large, dark ducks and geese generally have shorter necks and are more stout over-all.

Quick I.D.: smaller than a goose; sleek, dark plumage; long tail; small head; sexes similar. *Flight:* neck held straight. *Breeding:* white saddle patches; inconspicuous red throat pouch. **Size:** 25–28 in.

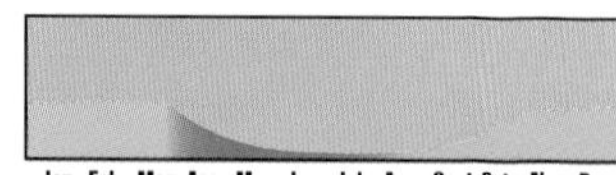

Great Blue Heron

Ardea herodias

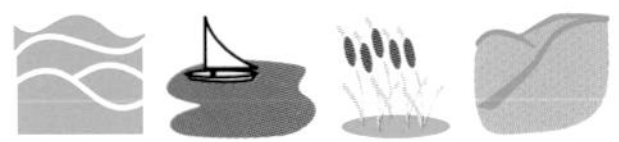

The Great Blue Heron is one of the largest and most regal of the coastal birds. It often stands motionless as it surveys the calm waters, its graceful lines blending naturally with the grasses and cattails of inland wetlands. All herons have specialized vertebrae that enable the neck to fold back over itself. The S-shaped neck, seen in flight, identifies all members of this wading family.

Hunting herons space themselves out evenly in favorite hunting spots, and they will strike out suddenly at prey below the water's surface. In flight, their lazy wingbeats slowly but effortlessly carry them up to their nests. These herons nest communally high in trees, building bulky stick nests that are sometimes in plain sight of urban areas.

The shallows of Puget Sound, Lake Washington, Union Bay and other, smaller wetlands often produce great numbers of this fascinating year-round resident.

Similar Species: None.

Quick I.D.: eagle-sized wing span; gray-blue plumage; red thighs; long, dagger-like, yellow bill; sexes similar.
Flight: head folded back; legs held straight back.
Size: 42–50 in.

Jan Feb Mar Apr May Jun Jul Aug Sept Oct Nov Dec

Green Heron

Butorides virescens

Jan Feb Mar Apr May Jun Jul Aug Sept Oct Nov Dec

Quick I.D.: crow-sized; small, stubby heron; short legs; glossy green back; chestnut throat; dark cap; sexes similar.
Breeding male: orange legs.
Immature: less colorful, with more streaking.
Size: 18–21 in.

This crow-sized heron is far less conspicuous than its great blue cousin. The Green Heron prefers to hunt for frogs and small fish in shallow, weedy wetlands, where it is often seen perched just above the water's surface. By searching the shallow, shady, overgrown wetlands edges in Juanita Bay, Marymoor Park and Lake Sammamish State Park, Seattle birders can often get a prolonged view of this otherwise reclusive bird.

The Green Heron often uses all of its tiny stature to hunt over a favorite site. With its bright yellow feet clasping a branch or reed, Seattle's smallest heron stretches nearly horizontal over water, its pose rigid and unchanging, until a fish swims into range. Like a taut bowstring, the tension mounts until the heron chooses to fire. Lunging its entire body at the prey, it is often soaked to the shoulders following a successful hunt.

Similar Species: American Bittern is larger, is heavily streaked and lacks any green color.

Virginia Rail

Rallus limicola

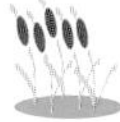

Quick I.D.: robin-sized; cinnamon breast; large feet; long, reddish bill; sexes similar.
Size: 9–10½ in.

To best experience a Virginia Rail, sit patiently alongside a marsh. The slim bird may reveal itself for an instant to a determined observer, but most often the bird's voice is all that betrays its presence. Telegraph-like ticks and a descending *wak-wak-wak-wak-wak* call are normally the only evidence of breeding Virginia Rails. If you are lucky, an April visit to Montlake Fill may be rewarded with the sounds or sightings of one of the few area breeders.

Virginia Rails build their raised nests in dense vegetation from cattails, bulrushes and sedges. They often add a roof and a runway to the nest if there is sufficient cover to hide the structure. Virginia Rails seldom leave their nesting marshes, and they are infrequently seen flying. Even when pursued by an intruder or predator, rails choose to scurry away through the dense protective vegetation rather than risk a getaway flight.

Similar Species: Sora has a black mask, dark body and short bill; Common Snipe (p. 65) has a longer bill, is heavily streaked and lacks the chestnut wing patch.

American Coot
Fulica americana

The American Coot has the lobed toes of a grebe, the bill of a chicken and the body shape and swimming habits of a duck. However, the American Coot is not remotely related to any of these species: its closest cousins are the rails and cranes. American Coots dabble, dive, walk on land, eat plant or animal matter and can be found in just about every freshwater pond, lake, marsh, lagoon or city park. These inland breeders retreat in great numbers to our mild coastal climates in the winter.

These loud, grouchy birds are seen chugging along in wetlands, frequently entering into short-lived disputes with other coots. American Coots appear comical while they swim: their heads bob in time with their paddling feet, and as a coot's swimming speed increases, so does the back and forth motion of its head. At peak speed, this motion seems to disorient the American Coot, and it will run, flap and splash towards the other side of the wetland.

Similar Species: All ducks and grebes generally lack the uniform black color and white bill.

Jan Feb Mar Apr May Jun Jul Aug Sept Oct Nov Dec

Quick I.D.: smaller than a duck; black body; white bill; red forehead shield; short tail; long legs; lobed feet; white undertail coverts; sexes similar.
Size: 15 in.

Brant

Branta bernicla

The local eelgrass beds spread out along the West Coast are like welcome truck stops for this small, dark marine goose. Thousands of migrating Brant move north in the spring along the exposed bars and sandflats of Puget Sound, on which they feed and preen. Scanning the shorelines from West Point or Alki Point during April will often reveal up to 50 birds fueling up for migration.

Brant, truly geese of the salt water, migrate exclusively to Alaska along the coast. Brant do not fly in tight 'V' formation: their flocks fly in wavy lines that frequently alternate between balling up and stretching out. When you encounter a flock during the spring along our shorelines, view the bird's delicate, lace-like throat markings and the flock's social behavior from a distance. Disrupting Brant that are feeding or resting often forces the geese to shuffle into the water and to drift away from their important daily activities.

Similar Species: Canada Goose (p. 30) is larger, and has white cheeks; Greater White-fronted Goose is brown over-all, with dark speckles on its breast; large ducks lack the black head and long black neck; cormorants (pp. 23–24) have black bellies and long, slender necks.

Quick I.D.: small goose; dark over-all; no white cheek; faint white necklace; white undertail coverts.
Size: 23–26 in.

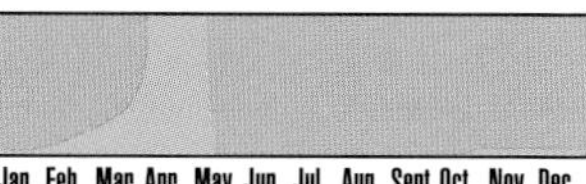

Canada Goose

Branta canadensis

Most flocks of Canada Geese in city parks and golf courses show little concern for their human neighbors. These urban geese seem to think nothing of creating a traffic jam or blocking a fairway while dining on lawns and gardens.

Breeding pairs mate for life, and not only will a widowed goose occasionally remain unpaired for the rest of its life, it's common for a mate to stay at the side of a fallen partner. Canada Geese are common throughout Seattle. Many subspecies migrate through the Pacific Northwest, and they can be recognized by the differences in size and color. Most Canada Geese seen around Seattle are of the large race from the Great Basin in eastern Washington. These pale-breasted birds were likely introduced into the Seattle region, where they have since established a large year-round breeding population.

Similar Species: Brant (p. 29) and large dabbling ducks are smaller and lack the white cheek; Greater white-fronted Goose lacks the white cheek and the black head and neck.

Quick I.D.: large goose; white cheek; black head and neck; brown body; white undertail coverts; sexes similar.
Size: 35–43 in.

Wood Duck

Aix sponsa

The male Wood Duck is one of the most colorful waterfowl in North America. Books, magazines, postcards and calendars routinely celebrate its beauty. No other duck can match this Seattle resident's iridescent, colorful and intricate plumage.

Wood Ducks nest in natural tree cavities or in nest boxes along ponds in the Snoqualmie River valley. The nests are usually found near water, and they may be 60 feet high in trees. The cavities themselves may contain as many as 12 eggs in a nest nestled among nothing more than down feathers. Following breeding, Wood Ducks often are found at Montlake Fill, where the males molt and lose all of their striking breeding plumage. Most species of duck enter this eclipsed stage for a brief period in late summer through fall, after which they normally once again molt into their breeding colors. The Wood Duck's species name, *sponsa*, is Latin for 'promised bride,' perhaps suggesting that the males appear all dressed up for a wedding.

Similar Species: Hooded Merganser (p. 46) has white patch on its crest and a slim bill; Harlequin Duck (p. 40) lacks a crest, and is blue-gray over-all.

Quick I.D.: small duck.
Male: glossy green head; crest slicked back from crown; white chin and throat; chestnut breast spotted white; white shoulder slash; golden sides; dark back and hindquarters.
Female: white teardrop eye patch; mottled brown breast streaked white; brown-gray upperparts; white belly.
Size: 19–20½ in.

Green-winged Teal

Anas crecca

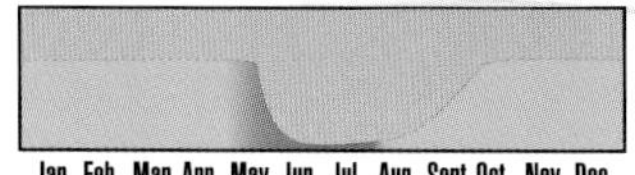

Quick I.D.: small duck; green wing patch; *Male:* chestnut head; green swipe trailing from eye; white vertical shoulder slash; gray body.
Female: mottled brown over-all.
Size: 14–16 in.

Although the Green-winged Teal nests on the prairies, it spends most of its life on the coast. One of the last ducks to leave Seattle in the spring and one of the first to return in the fall, the Green-winged Teal requires only a four-month stay to breed, nest, raise its many ducklings, and return home.

From August to April, this smallest North American dabbler is most often seen along cattail marshes on the edges of Lake Washington, Union Bay and the Kent Ponds. The small ducks prefer calm waters, where they as often as not shun the company of larger waterfowl and remain with their own kind. When Green-winged Teals take to the air, they are among the fastest of ducks, showing their green inner wing patches amid a blur of wingbeats.

Similar Species: Eurasian Teal lacks the white shoulder slash; American Wigeon (p. 36) has a white forehead and gray face; Eurasian Wigeon has a white forehead and lacks the green swipe; male Blue-winged Teal has a steel-blue head and a white crescent on his face; female Blue-winged Teal has a blue wing patch and lacks white undertail coverts.

Mallard
Anas platyrhynchos

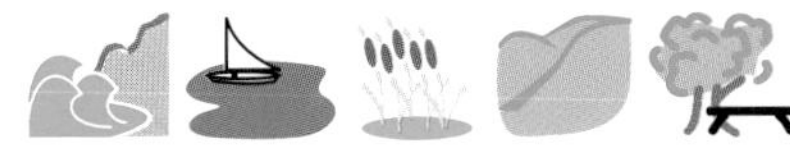

Quick I.D.: large duck; bright orange feet.
Male: iridescent green head; bright yellow bill; chestnut breast; white flanks.
Female: mottled brown; blue speculum bordered by white; bright orange bill marked with black.
Size: 22–26 in.

Jan Feb Mar Apr May Jun Jul Aug Sept Oct Nov Dec

The Mallard is the classic duck of inland marshes—the male's iridescent green head and chestnut breast are symbolic of wetland habitat. This large duck is commonly seen feeding in city parks, small lakes and shallow bays. With their legs positioned under the middle part of their bodies, Mallards walk easily, and they can spring into flight straight out of water without a running start. Mallards are the most common duck in North America (and the Northern Hemisphere), and they are easily seen year-round in Seattle. During the winter, flocks of Mallards are seen in open freshwater or grazing along shorelines. Because several species often band together in these loose flocks, birdwatchers habitually scan these groups to test their identification skills. Mallards (like all ducks) molt several times a year, so remember that the distinctive head of the male Mallard occasionally loses its green pizzazz.

Similar Species: Northern Shoveler (p. 34) has a green head, white breast and chestnut flanks; female Mallard resembles many other female dabbling ducks, look for the blue speculum and close association with the males.

Northern Shoveler

Anas clypeata

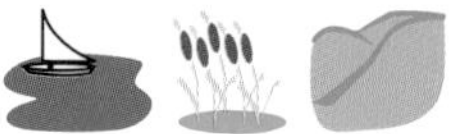

Quick I.D: medium-sized duck; large bill (longer than head width).
Male: green head; white breast; chestnut sides.
Female: mottled over-all; similar form to the male.
Size: 18–20 in.

The Northern Shoveler's shovel-like bill stands out among dabbling ducks. Its species name, *clypeata*, is Latin for 'furnished with a shield.' The comb-like structures along the bill's edges and its broad, flat shape allow the shoveler to strain small plants and invertebrates from the water's surface or from muddy substrates. A few Northern Shovelers breed in the Seattle region, but most of the birds seen in the winter reproduce far inland.

Many novice birders in Seattle become interested in birds because they realize the great variety of ducks in their city parks. Some ducks, like the Northern Shoveler, are dabblers that prefer shallow water, are not opposed to roaming around on land and lift straight off the water like a helicopter. Many ducks in the Seattle area are divers, confined to large lakes and saltwater bays where they can be seen running across the water to gain flight. Separating the divers from the dabblers is a first step into the wondrous world of waterfowl.

Similar Species: Mallard (p. 33) and all other dabbling ducks lack the combination of the large bill, white breast and chestnut sides.

Gadwall

Anas strepera

Quick I.D.: medium-sized duck; black-and-white wing patch (often seen in resting birds); white belly.
Male: mostly gray; black hindquarters.
Female: mottled brown.
Size: 19–21 in.

Among the flocks of ducks grazing calmly beside the shores of Lake Washington and Green Lake you can find our most unassuming species of waterfowl. At a quick glance, even a male Gadwall can pass for a female Mallard. During the Gadwall's elaborate courtship, however, its identity is completely clear. After a sign of interest from the female, the male raises his black hindquarters high out of the water, bobs his head and extends his wings, showing off the black-and-white speculum. Should the male's aquatic artistry meet the approval of the onlooking female, the pair may produce up to 11 eggs in a well-concealed nest.

As recently as the 1970s, Gadwall nesting records were considered unusual for the Northwest, but they have become a common sight in wetlands in all of Seattle's parks and open areas.

Similar Species: Female Mallard (p. 33) has a blue speculum; female Green-winged Teal (p. 32) has a green speculum and is smaller.

American Wigeon

Anas americana

During the winter, American Wigeons can easily be found and identified in the shallows and grassy shorelines of Seattle's ponds. The white top and gray sides of the male American Wigeon's head look somewhat like a balding scalp, while the nasal *wee-he-he-he* calls sound remarkably like the squeaks of a squeezed rubber ducky.

From mid-October through April, small non-breeding populations of this medium-sized duck are supplemented by thousands of wintering American Wigeons from the interior and the prairies. Occasionally mixed in with one of our most common North American dabblers is their Siberian counterpart, the Eurasian Wigeon. Hundreds of these Asian birds take a wrong turn at the Bering Sea and accidentally follow the American shoreline instead of the Asian one during their fall migration.

Similar Species: Eurasian Wigeon has a cinnamon head with no green swipe, a white forehead, and breeds in Asia; Green-winged Teal (p. 32) is smaller, has a rusty head with a green swipe, and a white shoulder slash.

Jan Feb Mar Apr May Jun Jul Aug Sept Oct Nov Dec

Quick I.D.: medium-sized duck; cinnamon breast and flanks; white belly; gray bill with black tip; green speculum.
Male: white forehead; green swipe running back from the eye.
Female: lacks distinct color on head.
Size: 18–21 in.

Canvasback

Aythya valisineria

Offshore in the bays of Lake Washington during the winter, a white-backed duck swims majestically, with its bill held high. Although at a distance birders can identify this bird as the stately Canvasback, binoculars or a spotting scope are usually required to closely study the duck's ruby eyes and rich mahogany head. Canvasbacks are ducks of the deep fresh waters, acquiring their vegetarian diet in well-spaced dives.

The Canvasback's distinctive profile results from the bird looking as though it has no forehead. The dark bill appears to run straight up to the top of the bird's head, providing the Canvasback with sleek and hydrodynamic-looking contours.

Redheads are ducks that are quite rare in Seattle, but are noteworthy in comparison to Canvasbacks. Like the Canvasback, the Redhead's head is ... red, but its back is gray and it has a forehead, just like that of a scaup.

Similar Species: Greater Scaup (p. 39) lacks the chestnut head and sloping forehead; Redhead (rare in Seattle) lacks the sloping forehead, and has a black-tipped bill and a darker back.

Quick I.D.: medium-sized duck; sloping bill and forehead.
Male: canvas-white back; chestnut head; black breast and hindquarters.
Female: brown head and neck; lighter body.
Size: 19–23 in.

Ring-necked Duck

Aythya collaris

Jan Feb Mar Apr May Jun Jul Aug Sept Oct Nov Dec

Quick I.D.: medium-sized duck; black bill tip; white bill ring.
Male: dark head with hints of purple; black breast, back and hindquarters; white shoulder slash; gray sides; white ring around base of bill; blue-gray bill with black-and-white banding on tip.
Female: dark brown body; light brown head; white eye-ring; lighter color closer to bill.
Size: 17 in.

In the Pacific Northwest, Ring-necked Ducks overwinter on wooded ponds and lakes from mid-September to mid-March. These diving ducks prefer ponds and lakes with muddy bottoms. Ring-necked Ducks dive deeply underwater for aquatic vegetation, including seeds, tubers and pondweed leaves, and for aquatic invertebrates. Because of their foraging habits, Ring-necked Ducks are susceptible to poisoning from ingesting lead shot; wasted shotgun pellets lie at the bottom of many wetlands in the Pacific Northwest.

Although this duck's name implies the presence of a collar, most experienced birders have given up on seeing this faint feature. The only prominent ring noticeable in field observation is around the tip of the bill, suggesting that a more reasonable name for this bird would have been the Ring-billed Duck.

Similar Species: Greater Scaup (p. 39) and Lesser Scaup lack the white shoulder slash and black back; female Redhead has a head that is the same tone as the body.

Greater Scaup

Aythya marilla

The Greater Scaup is the Oreo cookie of the coastal ducks—black at both ends and white in the middle. It is a diving duck that prefers deep, open water, and during the winter, it is common on lakes, harbors, estuaries and lagoons.

Most ducks seen in deep water are diving ducks, while those seen on shallow ponds or walking on land tend to be dabbling ducks. Diving ducks have smaller wings, which helps them underwater but makes for difficult takeoffs and landings. When a duck scoots across the water in an attempt to get airborne, even a first-time birder can tell it's a diver. Divers' legs are placed well back on their bodies—an advantage for underwater swimming, but not for easy walking. All ducks are front-heavy, so in order for diving ducks to stand, they must raise their front ends high to maintain balance. As a result of its diving adaptations, the Greater Scaup is clumsy on land and during takeoff, but it gains dignity in flight and on the water.

Similar Species: Lesser Scaup has a purplish tinge to its head; Ring-necked Duck (p. 38) has black back and white shoulder slash; Common Goldeneye (p. 43) and Barrow's Goldeneye (p. 44) lack the black neck.

Quick I.D.: medium-sized duck.
Male: dark, rounded head with hints of green; black breast and hindquarters; grayish-white sides and upperparts.
Female: dark brown; well-defined white patch at base of bill.
Size: 18 in.

Harlequin Duck

Histrionicus histrionicus

Jan Feb Mar Apr May Jun Jul Aug Sept Oct Nov Dec

Quick I.D.: medium-sized duck.
Male: blue over-all; white slashes on shoulder, neck and back; white spots on head and neck; chestnut flanks.
Female: brown over-all; white ear spot.
Size: 15–18 in.

Bobbing like colorful corks, Harlequin Ducks seem almost unsinkable—in spite of their preference for turbulent and chaotic habitats. During the winter, these ducks can be seen precariously close to breaking surf, but 'Harlies' seem unconcerned by their dangerous environment. The duck's rotund physique helps it navigate the torrents—small, rounded objects catch less of the counter-currents than do long and narrow forms. These ducks are regularly spotted during the winter as they forage off the coastline of West Point.

During the summer, most Harlequin Ducks leave the coast and go inland to seek out the most turbulent mountain streams. In these frothing waters, the drably colored female is left to raise the brood of ducklings. 'Harlequin' refers to a colorfully made-up actor.

Similar Species: Male is distinctive; females of Greater Scaup (p. 39), Lesser Scaup, Comon Goldeneye (p. 43) and Barrow's Goldeneye (p. 44) lack the ear spot; female Bufflehead (p. 45) is much smaller; White-winged (p. 41), Surf (p. 42) and Black scoters are larger and have foreheads that slope straight towards the bill tip.

White-winged Scoter

Melanitta fusca

As White-winged Scoters race across choppy winter seas, their flapping wings reveal their key diagnostic feature. The white inner wing patches strike a sharp contrast with the bird's otherwise all-black plumage and the dark waters. Scoters are heavy-bodied ducks that dive deeply, using both their feet and their partially spread wings, in foraging dives that last up to one minute or so. These large ducks form rafts on the offshore waters, where they dive for snails, mussels, clams and crustaceans. The gizzards of scoters are exceptionally strong, and they are capable of grinding these hard-shell invertebrates into digestible matter.

Black Scoters, the rarest of the three scoters, also occur in the Seattle region. These all-black birds winter on Puget Sound, and they are often seen in mixed-species rafts with the two other scoters.

Similar Species: Surf Scoter (p. 42) lacks the white wing patches, and has a white forehead and nape; Black Scoter is all black, with no white on its wings or head, and it has a bulbous orange bill.

Quick I.D.: large, stocky, dark duck; white wing patch; large bill; sloping forehead; base of bill is fully feathered.
Male: black over-all; white eye patch.
Female: brown over-all; gray-brown bill; light patches on cheek and ear.
Size: 20–23 in.

Surf Scoter

Melanitta perspicillata

Jan Feb Mar Apr May Jun Jul Aug Sept Oct Nov Dec

Quick I.D.: large duck.
Male: black over-all; white forehead, nape and base of bill; orange bill.
Female: dark brown; light cheek.
Size: 18–21 in.

Tough, big and stocky, scoters are more strong than graceful. Scoters are deep-diving sea ducks, and stormy weather amounts to nothing more than a simple annoyance in their feeding habits. Surf Scoters are frequently observed among white-capped waves. They dive to wrench shellfish from rocks with their sturdy bills, and they swallow the shellfish whole.

Surf Scoters form rafts in Puget Sound during the winter months. In the spring, these large black ducks migrate inland to lakes and tundra ponds as far north as Alaska and the Yukon. On the choppy sea, Surf Scoters live up to their name by 'scooting' across the water's surface, occasionally crashing through incoming waves.

Similar Species: White-winged Scoter (p. 41) has white wing patches and a white eye spot; Black Scoter has all-black plumage; other dark waterfowl lack the white forehead and white nape.

Common Goldeneye

Bucephala clangula

Quick I.D.: medium-sized duck.
Male: large, dark green to black head; round, white cheek patch; white body; black back streaked with white.
Female: chocolate-brown hood; sandy-colored body.
Size: 17–19 in.

Jan Feb Mar Apr May Jun Jul Aug Sept Oct Nov Dec

Although Common Goldeneyes don't breed in the Seattle area, they are extremely common from late fall right up to spring migration. Their courtship antics, staged on Puget Sound, Green Lake, Lake Washington and just about every other large body of water from winter through spring, reinforce a pair's bond prior to their migration to Canadian woodland lakes.

The courtship display of this widespread duck is one of nature's best slapstick routines. The spry male goldeneye rapidly arches his large green head back until his bill points skyward, producing a seemingly painful *kraaaagh*. Completely unaffected by his chiropractic wonder, he continuously performs this ritual to mainly disinterested females. The male continually escalates his spring performance, creating a comedic scene that is most appreciated by birdwatchers.

Similar Species: Hooded Merganser (p. 46), Bufflehead (p. 45) and Barrow's Goldeneye (p. 44) all lack the round, white cheek patch.

Barrow's Goldeneye

Bucephala islandica

Jan Feb Mar Apr May Jun Jul Aug Sept Oct Nov Dec

Quick I.D.: medium-sized duck.
Male: white crescent between eye and bill; white spots on back; dark head and back; white underparts.
Female: chocolate brown head; sandy body; yellow-orange bill (in spring).
Size: 17–19 in.

Only days old, small goldeneye chicks are lured out of their nest—an old woodpecker hole high in a tree—by their pleading mother. With a faith-filled leap, the cottonball ducklings tumble toward the ground, often bouncing on impact. When all the siblings have leapt into the waiting world, they follow their mother through the dense underbrush to the nearest water.

Much of the world's population of the Barrow's Goldeneye begins life by tumbling out of trees in Washington, Oregon and British Columbia. This species generally prefers saltwater to fresh during the winter, and it is often found around barnacle-encrusted rocks and pilings near piers and ferry terminals. This northwestern ducks bears the name of an Englishman who never visited the region. Sir John Barrow was an early 19th-century explorer intent on finding a passage through the Arctic. Although he never completed his lifelong mission, his name also graces a number of important Arctic landmarks.

Similar Species: Male Common Goldeneye (p. 43) lacks the white crescent and the white spots on his back; female Common Goldeneye has a darker bill.

Bufflehead

Bucephala albeola

Quick I.D.: tiny, round duck.
Male: white triangle on back of head; white body; dark back.
Female: dirty brown; small white cheek patch.
Size: 13–15 in.

The small, fluffy Bufflehead is perhaps the 'cutest' of Seattle's ducks: their simple plumage and rotund physique bring to mind a child's stuffed toy. During the winter, Buffleheads are found on just about every inland lake, pond and wetland in the Pacific Northwest. Although they are common in parks and urban ponds, Buffleheads (unlike many other duck species) rarely accept handouts from humans.

Because ducks spend most of their lives dripping with water, preening is an important behavior. At the base of the tail of most birds lies the preen (or uropygial) gland, which secretes a viscous liquid that inhibits bacterial growth and waterproofs and conditions feathers. After gently squeezing the oil gland with its bill, a bird can spread the secretion methodically over most of its body, an essential practice to revitalize precious feathers. Since sun and wind damage feathers, it is understandable that birds spend so much time preening and conditioning their feathers.

Similar Species: Males of Common Goldeneye (p. 43), Barrow's Goldeneye (p. 44) and Hooded Merganser (p. 46) are all larger and lack the white, unbordered triangle behind the eye; female Harlequin Duck (p. 40) is larger.

Hooded Merganser
Lophodytes cucullatus

The arrival of spring at Montlake Fill usually coincides with the courtship antics of a pair or two of Hooded Mergansers. Despite the male's remarkable, fully erect crest and his frog-like, seductive, slurring *crrrrooo*, prospective mates initially appear mainly disinterested. Out of seeming frustration, energetic male 'Hoodies' reach deep into their bags of courting tricks to perform a most unusual display: before a potential mate, the male routinely performs a complete somersault, taking off and landing perfectly on the water's surface.

Hooded Mergansers usually nest in cavities 15–20 feet up a tree. A large abandoned woodpecker cavity is often lined with leaves, grass and down, and the female alone incubates 10 to 12 white eggs. Once the ducklings hatch, they leap from their nest and stumble through the vegetation to the nearest wetland. Using the wetland as a nursery, the young Hooded Mergansers grow quickly, and they are usually flying within 70 days of hatching.

Similar Species: Bufflehead (p. 45) lacks the black outline to the crest and lacks the many white slashes.

Jan Feb Mar Apr May Jun Jul Aug Sept Oct Nov Dec

Quick I.D.: small duck; thin, serrated bill.
Male: black face; bold white crest outlined in black; white breast; white shoulder slash; golden-brown sides; black back.
Female: mottled brown over-all; shaggy reddish-brown crest.
Flight: black-and-white wing patches; flattened crests.
Size: 18 in.

Red-breasted Merganser

Mergus serrator

Quick I.D.: large duck.
Male: well-defined, dark green hood; punk-like crest; gray body; spotted, red breast; white collar; brilliant orange bill and feet; black spinal streak.
Female: rusty hood blending into white chest; gray body.
Size: 21–25 in.

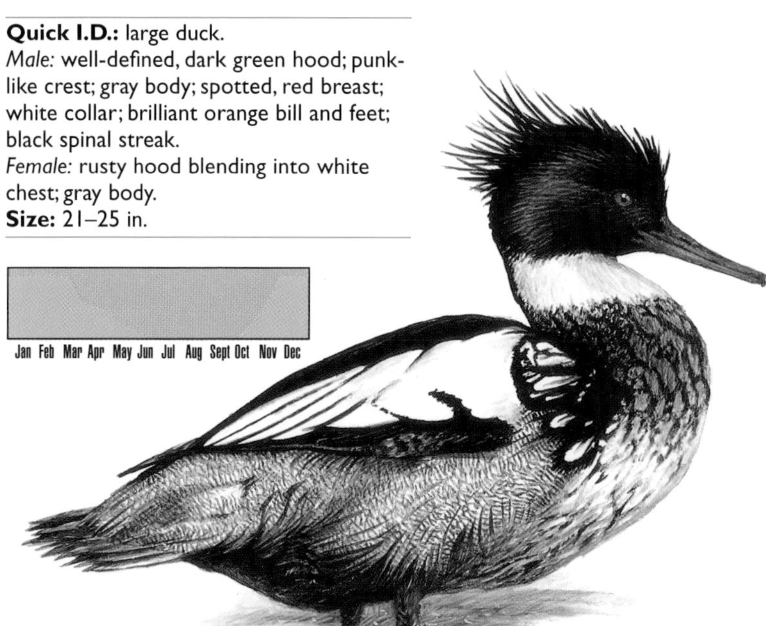

The Red-breasted Merganser runs along the surface of the water, beating its heavy wings, to build up sufficient speed for lift-off. Once in the air, this large duck looks compressed and arrow-like as it flies strongly in low, straight lines.

Mergansers are lean and powerful waterfowl designed for the underwater pursuit of fish. Unlike bills of other fishers, a merganser's bill is saw-like, serrated to ensure that its squirmy, slimy prey does not escape. Red-breasted Mergansers are found almost exclusively on saltwater in Seattle during the winter. Their quick 'fly bys' and flashing, white inner wing patches are common winter features off Alki and West points. On Shilshole Bay north of Discovery Park, flocks of up to 100 birds can be observed rafting offshore.

Common Mergansers are year-round residents in our area and a few nest along the Snoqualmie River. Unlike the Red-breasted Merganser, Common Mergansers tend to winter on freshwater lakes and rivers.

Similar Species: Male Common Merganser lacks the red breast and has white underparts; female Common Merganser has a well-defined, reddish-brown hood; large ducks and Common Loon (p. 18); all lack the combination of a green head, orange bill, orange feet and red breast.

Ruddy Duck

Oxyura jamaicensis

The clowns of freshwater wetlands, male Ruddy Ducks paddle energetically around their breeding wetlands, displaying with great vigor and beating their breasts with their bright blue beaks. The *plap-plap-plap-plap-plap* sound of their display speeds up until its climax—a spasmodic jerk and sputter. The male's performance occurs from May to the middle of June, and it can be seen easily at Montlake Fill.

The Ruddy Duck's winter demeanor contrasts sharply with its summer habits. The drably plumaged males lack their courting energy and their summer colors. These stiff-tailed diving ducks are found commonly during the non-breeding season offshore on Green Lake and Union Bay.

Similar Species: All other waterfowl are generally larger and have shorter tails and relatively smaller heads.

Jan Feb Mar Apr May Jun Jul Aug Sept Oct Nov Dec

Quick I.D.: small duck; broad bill; large head; tail often cocked up.
Breeding Male: reddish-brown neck and body; black head and tail; white cheek; blue bill.
Non-breeding Male: dull brown over-all; dark cap; white cheek.
Female: like non-breeding male, but pale cheek with dark stripe.
Size: 14–16 in.

Osprey

Pandion haliaetus

The Osprey is Seattle's 'sea hawk,' commonly seen over large waterbodies from April through September. A number of nesting sites occur in the Seattle area, and a short drive north to Port Gardner will provide an opportunity to easily observe these large raptors nesting on top of pilings.

To hunt, an Osprey surveys the calm water of a coastal bay from the air. Spotting a flash of silver at the water's surface, the Osprey folds its great wings and dives towards the fish. An instant before striking the water, the bird thrusts its talons forward to grasp its slippery prey. The Osprey may completely disappear beneath the water to ensure a successful capture; then it reappears, slapping its wings on the surface as it regains flight. Once it has regained the air, the Osprey shakes off the residual water and heads off toward its bulky stick nest, holding its prey facing forward.

Similar Species: Bald Eagle (p. 50) is larger, and never has the combination of white underparts and a white head with an eye streak; other large raptors are seldom seen near water.

Quick I.D.: smaller than an eagle; white underparts; dark elbow patches; white head; dark streak through the eye; sexes similar.
Flight: wings held in a shallow 'M.'
Size: 21–24 in.

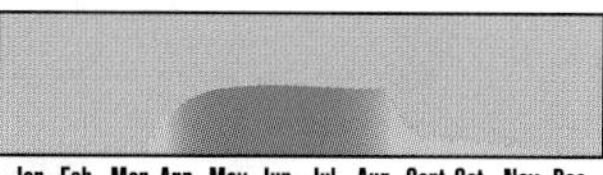

Bald Eagle
Haliaeetus leucocephalus

Salmon runs, concentrated waterfowl, washed-up carcasses and Osprey (from which to pirate food) ensure that West Coast Bald Eagles rarely go hungry. Bald Eagles are adept at catching fish, which they pluck from just below the water's surface, but America's national emblem is satisfied with a meal requiring less effort. As perhaps the nation's most regal scavengers, Bald Eagles serve a diverse ecological role.

The easy-living eagles spend much of their lives perched high in trees overlooking bays. A Bald Eagle takes four or five years to acquire its distinctive white tail and head, but younger birds are easily distinguished by their $6\frac{1}{2}$-foot wingspan. No one can help but appreciate the sight of a mature eagle spotted above downtown Seattle.

Similar Species: Osprey (p. 49) is smaller, with a black stripe through its white head; Turkey Vulture (uncommon vagrant), has a small, naked, red head and silver flight feathers, and its wings are often held in a shallow 'V.'

Quick I.D.: larger than a hawk; unmistakable, white head and tail; dark brown body and wings; yellow bill and talons.
Immature (1–5 years old): variable, but always large; mostly dark brown; certain plumages are heavily streaked in white.
Size: 35–40 in.

Jan Feb Mar Apr May Jun Jul Aug Sept Oct Nov Dec

Northern Harrier

Circus cyaneus

This common marsh hawk can best be identified by its behavior: the Northern Harrier traces wavy lines over lush meadows, often retracing its path several times in the quest for prey. Watch the slow, lazy wingbeats of the Northern Harrier coincide with its undulating, erratic flight pattern as this raptor skims the brambles and bulrushes with its belly. Unlike other hawks, which can find their prey only visually, the Northern Harrier stays close enough to the ground to listen for birds, voles and mice. When movement catches the Harrier's eyes or ears, it abandons its lazy ways to strike at prey with channeled energy.

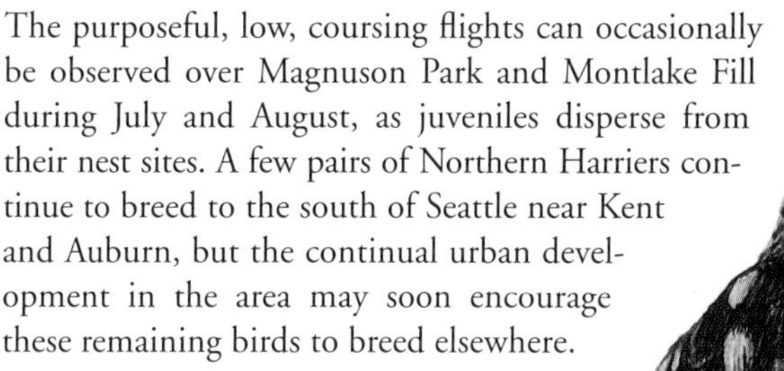

The purposeful, low, coursing flights can occasionally be observed over Magnuson Park and Montlake Fill during July and August, as juveniles disperse from their nest sites. A few pairs of Northern Harriers continue to breed to the south of Seattle near Kent and Auburn, but the continual urban development in the area may soon encourage these remaining birds to breed elsewhere.

Similar Species: Short-eared Owl (p. 82); Red-tailed (p. 53), Cooper's and Swainson's hawks all lack the white rump.

Quick I.D.: medium-sized hawk; white rump; long tail; long wings; parabolic face (noticeable only at close range).
Male: gray.
Female and *Immature:* brown over-all.
Size: 20 in.

Jan Feb Mar Apr May Jun Jul Aug Sept Oct Nov Dec

Sharp-shinned Hawk

Accipiter striatus

If songbirds dream, the Sharp-shinned Hawk is sure to be the source of their nightmares. 'Sharpies' pursue small birds through forests, passing by limbs and branches in the hope of acquiring prey. Sharp-shinned Hawks take more birds than other accipiters, with small songbirds and the occasionally woodpecker being the most numerous items. These small hawks are easy to find at Montlake Fill and Discovery Park as they pass through the area during their fall migration.

During the winter months, Sharp-shinned Hawks terrorize the songbirds living in Seattle's neighborhoods. Backyard feeders tend to concentrate finches, sparrows and juncos, so they are attractive foraging areas for these small hawks. A sudden eruption of songbirds off the feeder, and a few feathers floating on the wind are often the signs of a sudden, successful Sharp-shinned attack.

Similar Species: Cooper's Hawk is usually larger, and its tail is rounded; Merlin (p. 54) has pointed wings and rapid wingbeats, and lacks the red chest streaks.

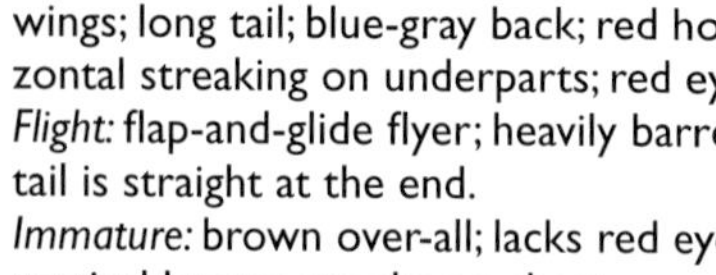

Quick I.D.: pigeon-sized; short, round wings; long tail; blue-gray back; red horizontal streaking on underparts; red eyes.
Flight: flap-and-glide flyer; heavily barred tail is straight at the end.
Immature: brown over-all; lacks red eye; vertical brown streaks on chest.
Size: 12–14 in. (female larger).

Jan Feb Mar Apr May Jun Jul Aug Sept Oct Nov Dec

Red-tailed Hawk

Buteo jamaicensis

With its fierce facial expression and untidy feathers, the Red-tailed Hawk looks as though it has been suddenly and rudely awakened. Its characteristic scream further suggests that the Red-tailed Hawk is a bird best avoided. You would think other birds would treat this large raptor with more respect, but the Red-tailed Hawk is constantly being harassed by crows, jays and blackbirds.

It isn't until this hawk is two or three years old that its tail becomes brick red. The black 'belt' around its midsection and the dark leading edge to its wings are better field marks because they're seen in most Red-taileds. Where the freeway south of Seattle passes through open country, it is difficult not to spot a Red-tailed perched upon a post or soaring lazily overhead.

Similar Species: Northern Harrier (p. 51) has a white rump; Cooper's Hawk is smaller, has a long tail and rarely soars; Rough-legged Hawk (uncommon winter migrant) has distinctive elbow patches.

Quick I.D.: large hawk; adult has brick-red tail; most plumages have a thin brown belt; light flight feathers with dark wing lining; sexes similar.
Size: 22 in.

Jan Feb Mar Apr May Jun Jul Aug Sept Oct Nov Dec

Merlin

Falco columbarius

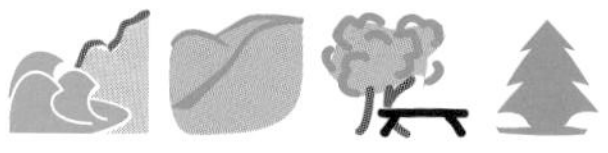

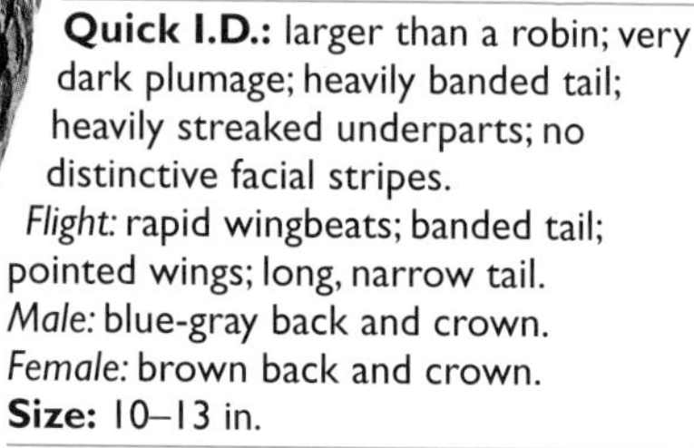

Quick I.D.: larger than a robin; very dark plumage; heavily banded tail; heavily streaked underparts; no distinctive facial stripes.
Flight: rapid wingbeats; banded tail; pointed wings; long, narrow tail.
Male: blue-gray back and crown.
Female: brown back and crown.
Size: 10–13 in.

Jan Feb Mar Apr May Jun Jul Aug Sept Oct Nov Dec

Like the sorcerer of King Arthur's court, the male Merlin wears a dapper blue cape upon his back. This small bird has few tricks in its hunting arsenal though, and like all its falcon relatives, its main weapons are speed and surprise. Merlins are highly specialized aerial hunters, and they prey on songbirds in Seattle's neighborhoods and parks. Their sleek body design, long, narrow tail and pointed wings are adaptations to maximize speed. The Merlin's loud and noisy cackling cry—*ki-ki-ki-ki-ki-kee*—is uttered in flight or while perched.

Merlins usually nest in conifers. They refashion the abandoned nests of crows, jays and some raptors. The nest is lined with sticks and feathers. Four or five eggs are incubated by either parent for up to 32 days. The young are carefully fed shreds of bird flesh by the parents until the young are strong enough to tear prey for themselves and begin flying, in about 35 days.

Similar Species: American Kestrel has two facial stripes; Peregrine Falcon (p. 55) has a distinctive dark hood, and is much larger; Sharp-shinned Hawk (p. 52) and Cooper's Hawk have short, round wings, and vertical streaking on the chest.

Peregrine Falcon

Falco peregrinus

The Peregrine Falcon is one of the fastest animals in the world: it can reach speeds of up to 100 mph. Once a Peregrine has its prey singled out, even the fastest ducks and shorebirds have little chance of escaping this effective predator. The Peregrine Falcon plunges on its prey, punching large birds in mid-air and following them to the ground, where they are killed and eaten.

The West Coast Peregrines have an abundant, pesticide-free, year-round food supply, and they do not need to migrate. Because they are not exposed to the same levels of pesticides as are migratory Peregrines, West Coast populations have not declined to the same degree as the inland birds. A few pairs breed along the wild, rocky shorelines, delighting and astonishing those who view their extraordinary hunting skills. Recently, Peregrine watchers have not needed to leave the city to view this exciting bird, as an active nest has been established atop the Washington Mutual Life Building in downtown Seattle.

Similar Species: Prairie Falcon has black 'wing pits' and is uncommon in Seattle; Gyrfalcon (winter vagrant) is much larger.

Quick I.D.: hawk-sized; dark blue hood extending down the cheek; steel-blue upperparts; light underparts with dark speckles; pointed wings; long tail. *Immature:* like adult except brown where adult is steel-blue; more heavily streaked underparts.
Size: 15–20 in.

Jan Feb Mar Apr May Jun Jul Aug Sept Oct Nov Dec

Ring-necked Pheasant

Phasianus colchicus

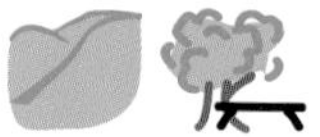

Quick I.D.: hawk-sized; long, tapering tail; short, round wings.
Male: iridescent green hood; fleshy red skin on cheeks; white necklace; golden-red body plumage.
Female: smaller than male; brown over-all.
Size: 31–35 in. (Male); 21–24 in. (Female).

Jan Feb Mar Apr May Jun Jul Aug Sept Oct Nov Dec

These spectacular birds, which were introduced from Asia, are common in dense, weedy fields in the Seattle region. The rooster-like *pe-cok* calls of male pheasants rise from brambles at Montlake Fill, surprising leisurely walkers.

During the breeding season, males collect a harem of up to five hens, which they then attempt to protect from the advances of rival males. Males are armed with a short but dangerous spur on the back of the leg, and fights between them can be fierce. Once males have mated with the harem, the females occasionally deposit their eggs into one communal nest. Whether overflowing with multiple clutches or not, pheasant nests are frequently preyed upon by Seattle's native fauna.

Similar Species: Male is distinctive; female Ruffed Grouse and Blue Grouse (p. 57) have shorter tails.

Blue Grouse

Dendragapus obscurus

In the dense montane forests of the Cascades, the Blue Grouse performs its annual courtship song in June. The male's voice is so deep that the human ear can hear only a fraction of the sounds. The low frequency travels well through the Cascade forest, however, and even our ears can hear the bird from as far away as 500 feet. The owl-like hooting attracts an audience of female Blue Grouse to the male's simple courtship dance.

The female displays its approval with another series of cackling notes. This auditory reinforcement is so stimulating to the males that they have been known to intimately investigate tape machines playing the female's response.

Similar Species: Ruffed Grouse is smaller, is gray-brown over-all, and has a dark tail band; Spruce Grouse is smaller, and has a black throat and breast.

Quick I.D.: hawk-sized; dark over-all; light gray tail tip.
Male: shows orange comb over eyes and yellow neck patch in courtship;
Female: mottled brown and gray.
Size: 19–21 in.

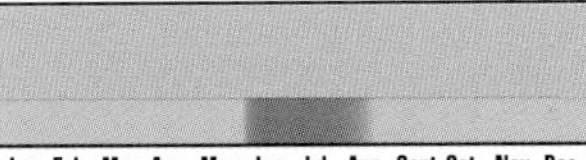

California Quail

Callipepla californica

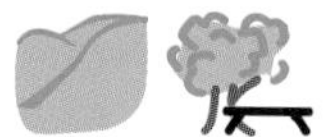

With its distinctive forward-facing plume, the California Quail looks like a flapper from the 1920s. California Quail scuttle around quickly, in tight, cohesive groups, and in most of Seattle's large parks, coveys are occasionally seen darting across paths in search of dense cover. Even when these shy birds refuse to leave their shrubby sanctuary, their noisy scratching and soft vocalizations betray their presence. During April and May, listen as the males advertise their courting desires by characteristically uttering *where are you*?

Similar Species: Mountain Quail is larger, and its plume rises straight back from its head; Ruffed, Blue (p. 57) and Spruce grouse are all larger and lack the forward-facing plume.

Jan Feb Mar Apr May Jun Jul Aug Sept Oct Nov Dec

Quick I.D.: robin-sized; forward-facing plume; gray-brown back; gray chest; white scales on belly; unfeathered legs.
Male: black throat; white stripes on head and neck.
Female: gray-brown face and throat.
Size: 10 in.

Killdeer

Charadrius vociferus

The Killdeer is probably the most widespread shorebird in the Pacific Northwest. It nests on gravely shorelines, utility rights-of-way, lawns, pastures and occasionally on gravel roofs within cities. Its name is a paraphrase of its distinctive loud call: *kill-dee kill-dee kill-deer*.

The Killdeer's response to predators relies on deception and good acting skills. To divert a predator's attention away from a nest or a brood of young, an adult Killdeer (like many birds) will flop around to feign an injury (usually a broken wing or leg). Once the Killdeer has the attention of the fox, crow or gull, it leads the predator away from the vulnerable nest. After it reaches a safe distance, the adult Killdeer is suddenly 'healed' and flies off, leaving the predator without a meal.

Similar Species: Semipalmated Plover has only one chest band, is smaller and is a migrant.

Quick I.D.: robin-sized; two black bands across breast; brown back; russet rump; long legs; white underparts; sexes similar.
Size: 9–11 in.

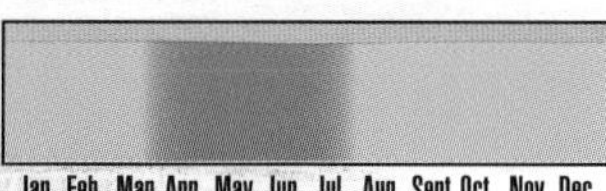

Greater Yellowlegs

Tringa melanoleuca

On a spring walk along the shorelines of Union Bay at Montlake Fill, you may see a few sandpipers. The Greater Yellowlegs prefers shallow pools where it can peck for small invertebrates, but it may venture belly-deep into water to pursue prey. Occasionally, a yellowlegs can be seen hopping along on one leg, with the other one tucked up in the body feathers to reduce heat loss.

Many birders enjoy the challenge of distinguishing the Greater Yellowlegs from the Lesser Yellowlegs. The Greater, which is more common on the West Coast (but don't let that bias your identification), has a relatively longer, heavier bill. The bill is also slightly upturned—so slightly that you notice it one moment and not the next. Generally, the Lesser calls with two *tews*, and the Greater calls with three. Cocky birders will name them at a glance, but more experienced birders will tell you that many of these people are bluffing, and that much of the time you can only write 'unidentified yellowlegs' in your field notes.

Similar Species: Lesser Yellowlegs is smaller, with a shorter bill; Sanderling (p. 62), Dunlin (p. 64) and Western Sandpiper (p. 63) are all much smaller and lack the yellow legs.

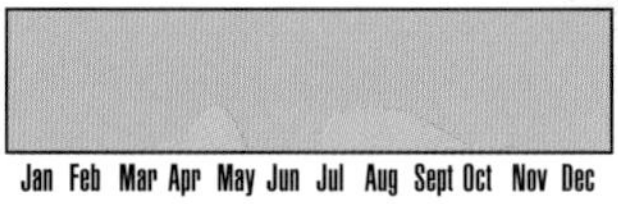

Jan Feb Mar Apr May Jun Jul Aug Sept Oct Nov Dec

Quick I.D.: smaller than a pigeon; long, bright yellow legs; finely streaked gray plumage; bill longer than head width; sexes similar.
Size: 13–15 in.

Spotted Sandpiper

Actitis macularia

This common shorebird of coasts, lakes and rivers has a most uncommon mating strategy. In a reversal of the gender roles of most birds, female Spotted Sandpipers compete for males in the spring. After the nest is built and the eggs are laid, the female leaves to find another mate, while the male incubates the eggs. This behavior is repeated two or more times before the female settles down with the last male to raise the chicks.

Spotted Sandpipers are readily identified by their arthritic-looking, stiff-winged flight low over water. Their peppy call—*eat-wheat wheat-wheat-wheat*—bursts from startled birds as they retreat from shoreline disturbances. Spotted Sandpipers are year-round residents of the Seattle area, but they are most frequently encountered during the summer months along the undisturbed shores of large waterbodies. Spotted Sandpipers constantly teeter and bob when not in flight, which makes them easy to identify.

Similar Species: Dunlin (p. 64) is usually seen in large flocks; Lesser Yellowlegs has long, yellow legs; Killdeer (p. 59) has dark throat bands.

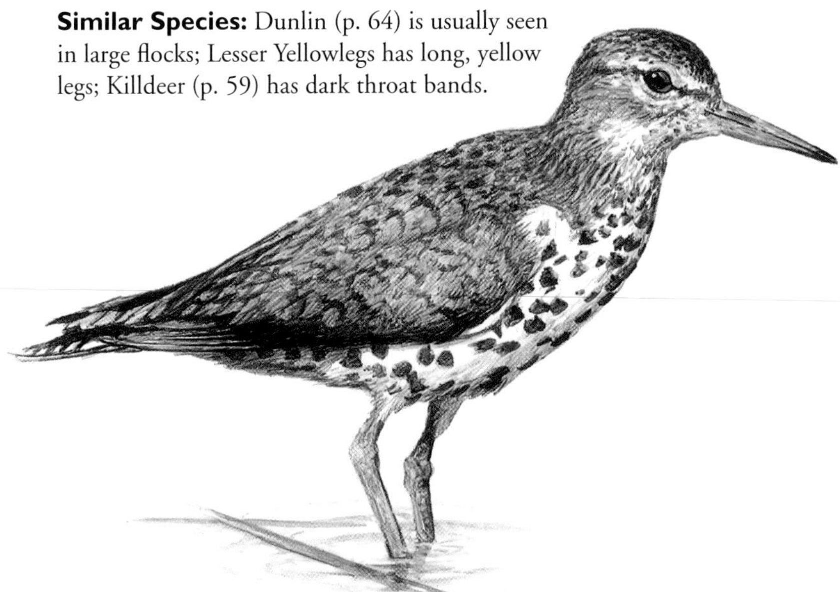

Quick I.D.: smaller than a robin.
Breeding: spotted breast; olive-gray back; often teeters; yellow legs; yellow bill tipped with black.
Female: spots more pronounced.
Size: 7–8 in.

Sanderling

Calidris alba

A winter stroll along a sandy saltwater beach is occasionally punctuated by the sight of these tiny runners. They appear to enjoy nothing more than playing in the surf. Sanderlings are characteristically seen chasing and retreating from the rolling waves, never getting caught in the surf. Only the Sanderling commonly forages in this manner, plucking at the exposed invertebrates stirred up by the wave action. Without waves to chase along calm shorelines, Sanderlings daintily probe into wet soil in much the same fashion as many other sandpipers.

This sandpiper is one of the world's most widespread birds. It breeds across the Arctic in Alaska, Canada and Russia, and it spends the winter running up and down sandy shorelines in North America, South America, Asia, Africa and Australia.

Similar Species: Western (p. 63), Least and Pectoral sandpipers are primarily migrants, and are smaller and darker; Dunlin (p. 64) is darker and has a downcurved bill.

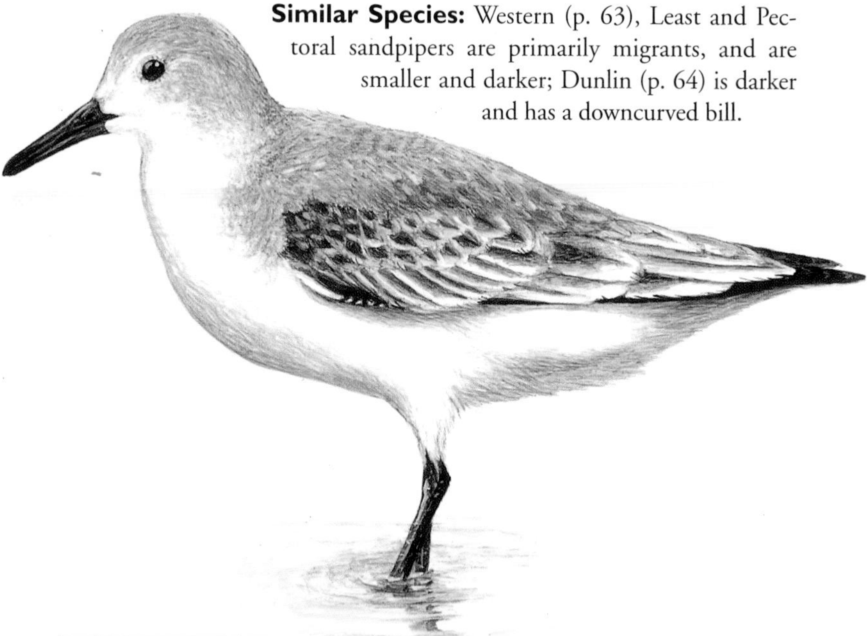

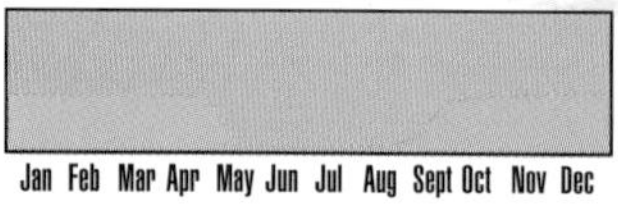

Jan Feb Mar Apr May Jun Jul Aug Sept Oct Nov Dec

Quick I.D.: smaller than a robin; straight, black bill; dark legs.
Non-breeding: white underparts; grayish-white upperparts.
Breeding (May): rusty head and breast.
Size: $7\frac{1}{2}$–$8\frac{1}{2}$ in.

Western Sandpiper

Calidris mauri

Wintering Western Sandpipers look nondescript, but what they lack in defining plumage they make up in numbers and synchrony. At migration times in the fall and spring, thousands of these shorebirds huddle and forage along open beaches, picking at the tiny organisms living in the damp shorelines.

The challenge of identifying wintering shorebirds awaits the interested birder at Montlake Fill. From July through September, many species of these confusing 'peeps' (as they are collectively called by birders) can be observed with patience, at very close range. Even if the subtlety of plumage is not your primary interest, a morning spent with shuffling sandpipers will prove to be enjoyable.

Similar Species: Sanderling (p. 62) is larger and frequently runs in the surf; Dunlin (p. 64) is larger and has more gray on its back; Semipalmated Sandpiper and Least Sandpiper are best separated in breeding plumage.

Quick I.D.: larger than a sparrow; black legs and bill. *Breeding:* rusty patches on crown, cheek, and wing. *Non-breeding:* grayish-brown upperparts; white eyebrow.
Size: 6–7 in.

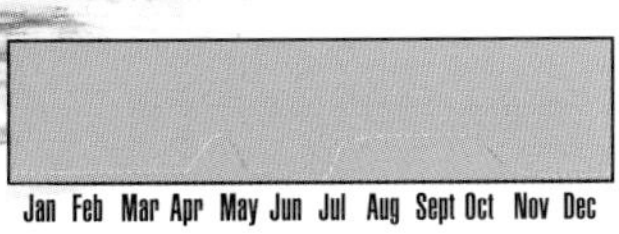

Jan Feb Mar Apr May Jun Jul Aug Sept Oct Nov Dec

Dunlin

Calidris alpina

The small, plump Dunlin is perhaps the most widespread winter shorebird in the Seattle area. Flocks of these birds can occasionally be seen on both fresh- and saltwater shorelines. Although the flocks move about continually around Seattle-area shorelines, Cedar River marsh and Lake Sammamish often host more than 2000 Dunlin through the winter. These tight flocks are generally more exclusive than many other shorebird troupes; few species mix with groups of Dunlin.

The Dunlin, like most other shorebirds, nests on the Arctic tundra and winters on the coasts of North America, Europe and Asia. It was first given the name Dunling (meaning 'a small brown bird'), but for reasons lost to science the 'g' was later dropped.

Similar Species: Western (p. 63), Least and Pectoral sandpipers are primarily migrants; Sanderling (p. 62) is smaller and paler, and is usually seen running in the surf.

Jan Feb Mar Apr May Jun Jul Aug Sept Oct Nov Dec

Quick I.D.: smaller than a robin; slightly downcurved bill; dark legs.
Non-breeding: pale gray underparts; grayish-brown upperparts.
Breeding (April–May): black belly; streaked underparts; rusty back.
Size: 9 in.

Common Snipe

Gallinago gallinago

Common Snipe have startled many walkers as they stroll through Montlake Fill and other Seattle-area marshes. These shorebirds are both secretive and well camouflaged, so few people notice them until the birds fly suddenly out of nearby grassy tussocks. As soon as snipe take to the air, they perform a series of quick zigzags, an evasive maneuver designed to confuse predators.

Snipe are seldom seen in large groups, nor are they normally encountered along open shorelines; their heavily streaked plumage is suited to grassy habitat. Because snipe do not commonly nest in the Seattle area, it is always a special treat when a spring or fall bird is heard 'winnowing.' This mystical sound, produced in flight by air passing through spread tail feathers, is heard only periodically, but often enough so that the thrill of each experience is never lost.

Similar Species: All other shorebirds are either too short of bill or not as heavily streaked.

Quick I.D.: robin-sized; long, black-tipped bill; heavily streaked back; short neck; striped head; long legs; sexes similar.
Size: 10½–11½ in.

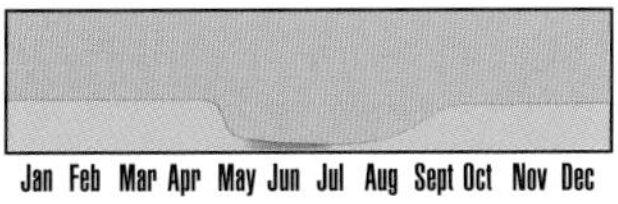

Jan Feb Mar Apr May Jun Jul Aug Sept Oct Nov Dec

Red-necked Phalarope

Phalaropus lobatus

Red-necked Phalaropes spin and whirl in shallow water during their migratory stopovers in Seattle, displaying an unexpected foraging technique for a shorebird. These small shorebirds land on the water and swim in tight circles, stirring up tiny crustaceans and quickly picking at the water's surface with their needle-like bills. These habitual spinners are best seen in the fall, from ferries that go across Puget Sound. Not only do Red-necked Phalaropes display unusual feeding strategies, but these most colorful of the shorebirds also exhibit breeding habits that are extremely rare through the entire animal kingdom. On their tundra nesting grounds, these migrants practice a mating strategy known as polyandry—the females mate with several males. The brightly colored female phalarope defends the nest site from other females, and it is her mate who incubates the eggs and rears the young.

Similar Species: Wilson's Phalarope (summer visitor) has a lighter head and back, and its flanks are unspotted.

Quick I.D.: robin-sized; thin black bill; long black legs; white wing stripe.
Breeding Female: chestnut neck and throat; white chin; blue-black head; incomplete, white eye-ring; white belly; buff stripes on upper wings; spotting on flanks.
Breeding Male: white eyebrow; less intense colors than the female.
Non-breeding (both sexes): white underparts; gray-blue upperparts; black mask extends from eye; white streaks on back.
Size: 7–8 in.

Jan Feb Mar Apr May Jun Jul Aug Sept Oct Nov Dec

Bonaparte's Gull

Larus philadelphia

The scratchy little calls of Bonaparte's Gulls accompany these winter residents as they forage along the Puget Sound waterfront. These gulls commonly feed on the water's surface, and they can often be seen resting atop concrete diving platforms. After spending the winter months on Puget Sound, most Bonaparte's Gulls leave the coast for the summer to breed in the northern boreal forest, where they nest, in most un-gull-like fashion, in spruce trees.

Outside the summer breeding season, most Bonaparte's Gulls lose their distinctive black hoods, but they retain flashy white wing patches and a noticeable black spot behind the eyes. This gull was named not after the famed French emperor, but after his nephew, Charles Lucien Bonaparte, who brought recognition to his family's name through the practice of ornithology.

Similar Species: Mew Gull (p. 68) lacks a black ear spot and is larger; Common Tern (p. 71) has a forked tail and lacks a white wing flash.

Quick I.D.: small gull; black bill; dark eye; wingtips have black outline; wings flash white in flight; sexes similar.
Breeding: black hood.
Non-breeding: white head with a dark ear spot.
Size: 12–14 in.

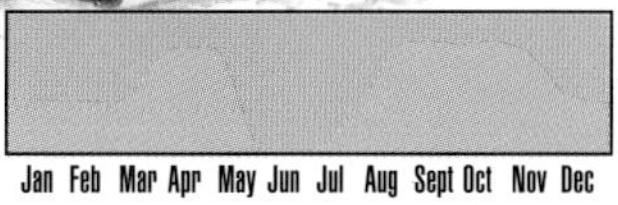

Jan Feb Mar Apr May Jun Jul Aug Sept Oct Nov Dec

Mew Gull

Larus canus

The Mew Gulls that overwinter along Puget Sound are not regular visitors to the local landfills. These small gulls, named after one of their calls, forego quick and convenient human leftovers for natural foods. Mew Gulls can be seen foraging in the Sound, frequently landing on the water to pick up floating matter. A Mew Gull will occasionally plunge its head beneath the water, but it seldom dives. These gulls are seen commonly on land only during heavy winter rains, when they feed in large numbers on park lawns. These common winter visitors nest in northern British Columbia, Alaska and Siberia.

Like other marine birds, the Mew Gull has specialized glands that lie around the eyes near the base of the bill to help it cope with the salt it ingests when drinking salt water. The glands extract salt from the blood and produce a concentrated salty liquid that can be seen dripping from the bill.

Similar Species: California, Glaucous-winged (p. 70), Herring, Ring-billed (p. 69), Western and Thayer's gulls are all much larger; Bonaparte's Gull (p. 67) has a black hood or ear patch and a white flash in the wings.

Quick I.D.: small gull; white head and body; light gray wings; black wingtips; yellow legs; dark eyes; sexes similar.
Size: 16–18 in.

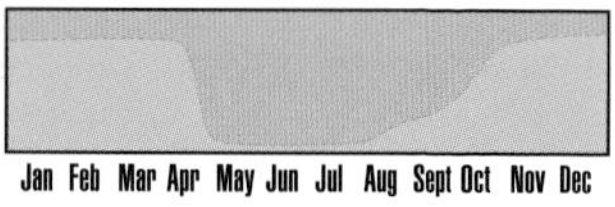

Jan Feb Mar Apr May Jun Jul Aug Sept Oct Nov Dec

Ring-billed Gull

Larus delewarensis

As August rolls through the Seattle area, Ring-billed Gulls return from their nesting sites on the Great Plains to overwinter along the coast. These medium-sized gulls do not make up a majority of the gull flocks in Seattle, but their bills are sufficiently distinctive to set them apart from the more numerous species in the area. The black ring around both the upper and lower mandible does not reach the bill's tip, which is as yellow as the rest of the bill.

During the winter, Ring-billed Gulls can be encountered throughout the entire Seattle region. They associate with other flocks of gulls in city parks, shopping center parking lots, fast food restaurants, and on lakes and ponds. They can occasionally be seen along the shorelines of Puget Sound. Along these beaches, Ring-billed Gulls eat dead fish, birds and other animal matter, while inland they take worms, garbage and waste grain.

Similar Species: Glaucous-winged Gull (p. 70) has a dark eye, lacks the bill ring, is much larger and has pink legs and gray wingtips; California Gull is larger, lacks the bill ring and has a dark eye; Herring Gull is larger, has pink legs and lacks the bill ring; Mew Gull (p. 68) has a dark eye and an all-yellow bill without a ring.

Quick I.D.: medium-sized gull.
Non-breeding: white head and nape washed with brown; yellow bill and legs; black ring near bill tip; dark gray wing covers; light eye; black wingtips; small white spots on black primaries; white underparts; sexes similar.
Immature: mottled grayish brown.
Size: 18–20 in.

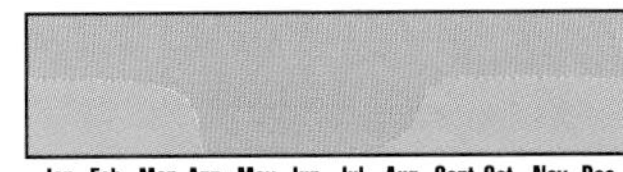

Glaucous-winged Gull

Larus glaucescens

Many gulls come and go in the Seattle area, but the Glaucous-winged Gull is a year-round resident. The Glaucous-winged Gull can truly be found anywhere and everywhere in Seattle as it has been able to adapt readily to the urbanization of the region. Large flocks of this gull can be found in bays, estuaries, freshwater lakes, garbage dumps, city parks and agricultural fields. Glaucous-winged Gulls are so widely dispersed they are sure to be sighted on just about any birding trip taken along the Puget Sound shoreline.

A very similar species, the Western Gull, becomes increasingly common in southern Washington, Oregon and California. Many hybrids of the two species live in the Seattle area; they look very much like pure Glaucous-wings except that their wingtips are dusky.

A rewarding exercise for novice birdwatchers is to glance over a flock of 50 or so birds. Within a few minutes, even the most inexperienced birder will begin to sort out the gulls based on their size and on the color of their eyes, wingtips and legs.

Similar Species: Herring Gull has pink feet, yellow eyes and black wingtips; California Gull and Ring-billed Gull (p. 69) have black wingtips and yellow-green feet; Western Gull has a dark back and wings, a yellow eye and black wingtips.

Jan Feb Mar Apr May Jun Jul Aug Sept Oct Nov Dec

Quick I.D.: large gull; white head and body; pale gray wingtips; light gray back and wings; pink legs; dark eyes; red spot on lower mandible; sexes similar.
Immature and *Non-breeding:* variable.
Size: 24–27 in.

Common Tern

Sterna hirundo

Wheeling about in mid-air to a stationary hover, the Common Tern carefully measures up its task and then dives quickly into the water. The headfirst dive is often rewarded with a small fish, which is carried away in the bird's thin bill. Common Terns migrate through Puget Sound mainly during the fall, stopping along the west coast to plunge after schools of small fish. Their effortless flight, bouncing lazily up and down in the rhythm of their wingbeats, is best seen at West Point and Shilshole Bay, from August through October.

Terns superficially resemble gulls in body form, but their behavior differs dramatically. Terns rarely soar in the air, and they are infrequently seen resting on the water or on the ground. While flying, terns usually have their bills pointed towards the ground, and their forked tails are usually visible. Common Terns lose most of their black breeding caps before their fall passage; they appear to have pattern baldness, as the black is restricted to the sides and back of the bird's head.

Similar Species: Caspian Tern is much larger and has a heavy, red bill and black legs; Arctic Tern (rare in migration) lacks the black-tipped bill and has a deeply forked tail and light primaries.

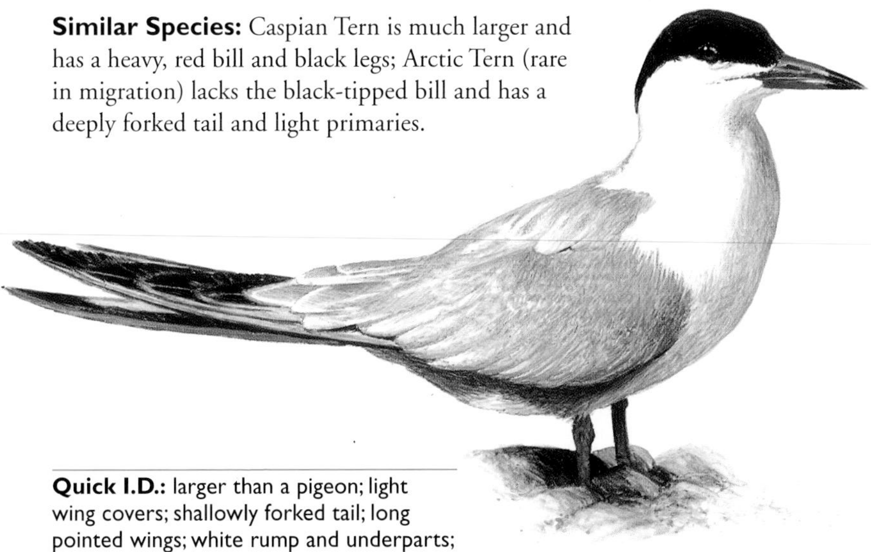

Quick I.D.: larger than a pigeon; light wing covers; shallowly forked tail; long pointed wings; white rump and underparts; mostly white tail; sexes similar.
Non-breeding: white forehead; black nape; black shoulder bar.
Breeding: black cap; red bill tipped with black.
Size: 14½ in.

Common Murre

Uria aalge

Like all alcids, Common Murres appear more comfortable on the sea than in the air. Their tiny wings are designed for pursuing fish underwater, and in flight they beat the air feverishly, attempting to maintain speed. Like uncontrolled missiles, murres veer from side to side as they rocket across Puget Sound. During the fall and winter, Common Murres can be seen flying offshore past Alki Point or West Point, and occasionally they can be closely observed as they drift with the current not far from shore.

Many birds that live on saltwater share the countershading coloration of the murre. From above, the dark back blends with the steely sea, while submerged predators and prey cannot find the light-colored underbelly against the bright sky. Unfortunately, gill nets lying hidden below the ocean surface claim many of these large alcids each year.

Similar Species: All other alcids and sea ducks lack the combination of a long, slender bill and distinctive countershading; Western Grebe (p. 21) has a long, slim neck; Horned Grebe (p. 20) is smaller and has a longer neck.

Jan Feb Mar Apr May Jun Jul Aug Sept Oct Nov Dec

Quick I.D.: crow-sized; sexes similar.
Breeding: black head and neck; black upperparts; white underparts.
Non-breeding: white neck and chin, otherwise similar.
Size: 16–17 in.

Pigeon Guillemot

Cepphus columba

Pigeon Guillemots are common seabirds that forage near shore and nest on rocky cliff ledges. The solid black breeding plumage surrounding a white wing patch is offset by the guillemot's radiant red mouth-lining and feet. These scarlet accents are flaunted outrageously during courtship rituals, when guillemots wave their feet and then peer down the throats of potential mates. The bold markings enable birdwatchers to easily spot Pigeon Guillemots nesting on brown cliffs.

Guillemots often roost on downtown piers, and they have nested on the south bluff of Discovery Park. Outside the nesting season, they are frequently seen riding the waves in Puget Sound.

Similar Species: Ancient Murrelet and Marbled Murrelet (p. 74) are smaller and lack the white wing patch; Western Grebe (p. 21) is larger, with a longer neck and black upperparts; Rhinoceros Auklet (p. 75) has a more robust body form and a thick bill, and lacks the white wing patch; Horned Grebe (p. 20) lacks the white wing patch.

Quick I.D.: pigeon-sized; bright red feet and mouth; white wing patch; long neck; sexes similar.
Breeding: black over-all.
Non-breeding: light head and underparts; dark back.
Size: 12–14 in.

Marbled Murrelet

Brachyramphus marmoratus

The Marbled Murrelet outsmarted the greatest North American ornithologists for over a century. Scientists were unable to find a single nest until 1974, when an attentive amateur discovered that this stubby seabird, far more adapted to life in the open water, nests 200 feet up, on mossy tree limbs. Its grouse-like breeding plumage should have been a major clue in the mystery. The Marbled Murrelet is dependent on coastal old growth, and it is declining as a direct result of logging practices, an almost inconceivable notion for a bird that spends 10 months of the year drifting at sea.

Although it is an endangered species, the Marbled Murrelet winters in reliable numbers in Puget Sound, and West Point offers Seattle naturalists an opportunity to view this bird. Murrelets are usually seen in pairs, and in flight their 'barrel roll' action separates them from direct-flying Ancient Murrelets. Recently, fledged young Marbled Murrrelets have been occasionally spotted on Puget Sound. As these young birds have obviously not traveled far, hidden murrelet nests must surely dot the Seattle area.

Similar Species: Common Murre (p. 72) is much larger and lacks the light stripe on the back; Ancient Murrelet has a white stripe over the eye and lacks the light stripe on the back.

Jan Feb Mar Apr May Jun Jul Aug Sept Oct Nov Dec

Quick I.D.: robin-sized; stocky; very short neck.
Breeding: mottled brown plumage; white eye-ring.
Non-breeding: dark upperparts; white underneath; white lines on back seen in flight.
Size: 9–10 in.

Rhinoceros Auklet

Cerorhinca monocerata

Over most of Puget Sound, the Rhinoceros Auklet is among the most common of the overwintering alcids. Built like a linebacker, this auklet has an overall bulky appearance, and it appears to have no neck. Rhinoceros Auklets drift confidently among winter squalls, seemingly unaware of the chilling wind and spray. Although these small oceanic birds can be viewed from lookouts along Puget Sound, one of the best places to meet robust Rhinos is at Edmond's fishing pier just south of the ferry terminal. During the winter, these stocky seabirds can be seen catching fish directly below the pier.

It is only during the breeding period (February to June) that this common auk sports its namesake horn. Most Rhinos leave Puget Sound for breeding colonies during March, only to return en masse in October, usually without their bill adornment.

Similar Species: Cassin's Auklet is much smaller, and it has a smaller bill; Marbled Murrelet (p. 74) and Ancient Murrelet are smaller and have white underparts.

Quick I.D.: smaller than a duck; dark brown upperparts; grayish-brown underparts; stout bill; short neck; sexes similar.
Breeding: yellow horn at base of bill; white plumes descending from eye and bill.
Size: 15 in.

Jan Feb Mar Apr May Jun Jul Aug Sept Oct Nov Dec

Rock Dove
Columba livia

The Rock Dove (or pigeon) is very dependent on humans for food and shelter. This Eurasian native lives in old buildings, on ledges and on bridges, and it feeds primarily on waste grain and human handouts.

Rock Doves may appear strained when walking—their heads move back and forth with every step—but few birds are as agile in flight, or as abundant in urban and industrial areas. While no other bird varies as much in coloration, all Rock Doves, whether white, red, blue or mixed-pigment, will clap their wings above and below their bodies upon takeoff.

Similar Species: Band-tailed Pigeon (p. 77) is larger, it has a grayish tail band, and it lacks the white rump; Mourning Dove is the same length, but it is slender, with a long, tapering tail and olive-brown plumage.

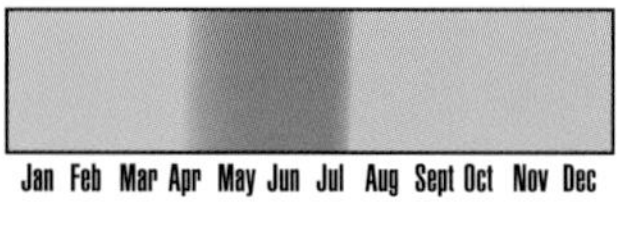

Jan Feb Mar Apr May Jun Jul Aug Sept Oct Nov Dec

Quick I.D.: medium-sized pigeon; color variable, iridescent blue-gray, black, red and white; usually has white rump; orange feet; fleshy base to the bill; sexes similar.
Size: 13–14 in.

Band-tailed Pigeon

Columba fasciata

Band-tailed Pigeons can be seen flying over Seattle's neighborhoods every day of the year, but few people take note of them since they appear so similar to Rock Doves. Band-tails are our native pigeon, and these secretive birds appear bulkier in flight than their ubiquitous and introduced counterpart. During the breeding season, individual birds are seen as 'fly-bys,' and they flock together only while feeding or roosting in trees.

Band-tailed pigeons are awkward feeders, as can be observed in many of our forested city parks and golf courses. The birds cling clumsily to branches that bend under their weight. As the pigeons yo-yo up and down, they carefully pluck at the fruits of the Pacific madrone, which they find particularly appealing. Band-tails also visit backyard feeders in the early morning hours, usually cleaning them out before the homeowner awakes. Band-tailed Pigeons nest in Seattle's neighborhoods, building their well-concealed nests among the upper branches of Douglas-fir trees.

Similar Species: Rock Dove (p. 76) is slightly smaller, has orange legs and usually has a white rump.

Quick I.D.: large pigeon; purple head and chest; white band at base of neck; grayish band on tail; rump not white; yellow bill tipped with black; sexes similar.
Size: 14–15½ in.

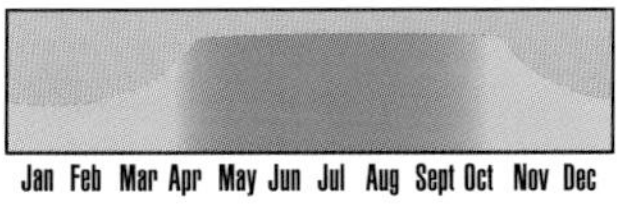

Jan Feb Mar Apr May Jun Jul Aug Sept Oct Nov Dec

Barn Owl
Tyto alba

Barn Owls and humans have gradually entered into a mutually beneficial relationship. Before European colonization, barn owls nested primarily in snags, hollow trees and caves, and they hunted voles and mice in shrublands. With the arrival of Europeans and their rodent associates (house mice and black rats), however, the diet of Barn Owls underwent a slight shift. Barn Owls now commonly roost in old buildings and barns as well as in natural cavities. They hunt the non-native rodents, much to the delight of present-day residents who view the rodents as agricultural and esthetic pests. Barn Owls have not been a complete benefactor of urbanization; some die each year in vehicular accidents and from human usage of pesticides.

Similar Species: None.

Quick I.D.: crow-sized; white, heart-shaped face; dark eyes; light underparts; golden-brown upperparts; sexes similar.
Size: 16 in.

Western Screech-Owl

Otus kennicottii

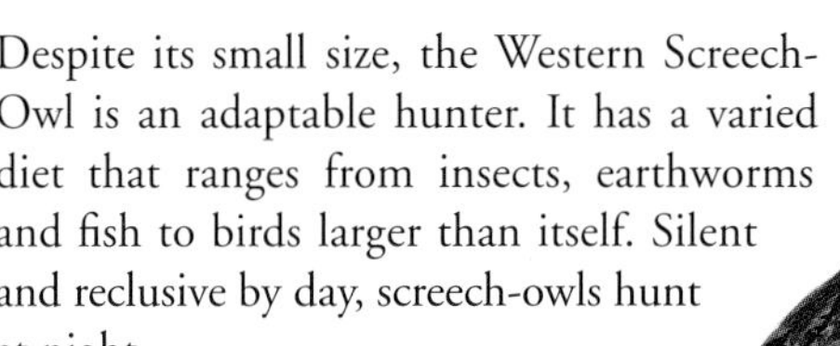

Despite its small size, the Western Screech-Owl is an adaptable hunter. It has a varied diet that ranges from insects, earthworms and fish to birds larger than itself. Silent and reclusive by day, screech-owls hunt at night.

Some owls' senses are refined for darkness and their bodies for silence. Their large, forward-facing eyes have many times more light-gathering sensors than do ours, and the wings of nocturnal owls are edged with frayed feathers for silent flight. Their ears, located on the sides of their heads, are asymmetrical (one is higher than the other), enabling these birds to track sounds more easily.

Given these adaptations, it is no surprise that owls have successfully invaded nearly all of the world's major ecosystems. Strolling along the wooded paths of Seattle's larger wooded parks (e.g., Seward, Schmitz or Lincoln) during early spring evenings, a person with a keen ear will hear the distinctive whistled voice of the Western Screech-Owl. The call's rhythm has often been compared to that of a bouncing ball coming to rest.

Quick I.D.: robin-sized; short ear tufts; heavy vertical streaking on chest; yellow eyes; dark bill; sexes similar.
Size: 8–9 in. (females slightly larger).

Similar Species: Northern Saw-whet Owl has a dark facial disc and no ear tufts, and its call does not increase in pace.

Great Horned Owl

Bubo virginianus

The Great Horned Owl is the most widely distributed owl in North America, and it is among the most formidable of coastal predators. It uses specialized hearing, powerful talons and human-sized eyes during nocturnal hunts for mice, rabbits, quail, amphibians and occasionally fish. It has a poorly developed sense of smell, which is why it can prey on skunks. Worn-out and discarded Great Horned Owl feathers are therefore often identifiable by a simple sniff.

The deep, resonant hooting of the Great Horned Owl is easily imitated, often leading to interesting exchanges between bird and birder. The call's deep tone is not as distinctive as its pace, however, which closely follows the rhythm of *eat my food, I'll-eat yooou.*

Similar Species: Spotted, Barred (p. 81) and Great Gray owls all lack ear tufts; Western Screech-Owl (p. 79) is much smaller and has vertical breast streaking; Long-eared Owl has a slimmer body with vertical streaks on its chest, and its ear tufts are very close together.

Quick I.D.: hawk-sized; large, widely spaced ear tufts; fine, horizontal chest bars; dark brown plumage; white throat; sexes similar.

Size: 18–25 in.

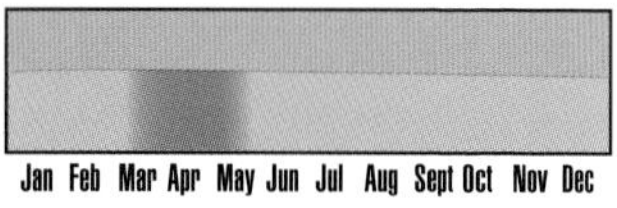

Jan Feb Mar Apr May Jun Jul Aug Sept Oct Nov Dec

Barred Owl

Strix varia

Spring nights in the coastal woods, and occasionally within the city limits, echo with the eerie call of the Barred Owl. The distinctive *who cooks for you, who cooks for you all?* is easily imitated, and the thrill of joining in the chorus is most memorable. But take care: your voice can be perceived as a threat, and it may provoke a spirited attack from nesting or hunting birds.

In our region, the Barred Owl can be found along steep-sloped ravines and bluffs with a mixedwood canopy. This species, which calls throughout the year, has bred for many years in the forests of Discovery Park, and it can also be found at Saint Edward State Park in nearby Kirkland.

Similar Species: Spotted Owl has spotting (not streaking) on its chest and body, its plumage is dark brown, and its call is not as complex.

Quick I.D.: larger than a crow; dark eyes; horizontal streaking on throat; vertical streaking on chest; sexes similar.
Size: 17–24 in. (females larger).

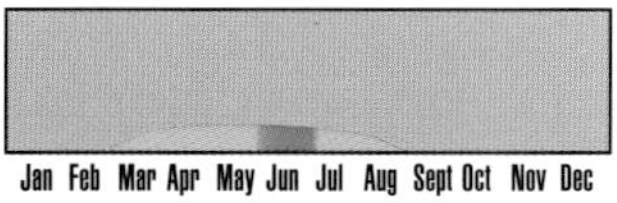

Jan Feb Mar Apr May Jun Jul Aug Sept Oct Nov Dec

Short-eared Owl

Asio flammeus

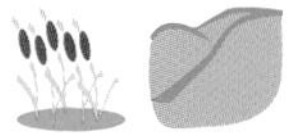

The Short-eared Owl's deep, lazy flapping makes it look more like a giant bat than like a bird. Near dawn and dusk, this predator of voles and mice is seen perched on fenceposts or flying over grassy meadows and marshes, searching for prey.

This owl's name is quite misleading, because its 'ears' (actually nothing more than feather tufts) are so short that they're rarely seen.

The Short-eared Owl is found throughout most of the world, but it is quickly losing nesting and foraging habitat in the Seattle area. As fields and meadows are developed, the Short-eared Owl is increasingly pushed out of our area. It is occasionally seen in the fall at Montlake Fill, and it often winters in small numbers at Magnuson Park.

Similar Species: Female and immature Northern Harriers (p. 51) have a white rump and a small head; Barn Owl (p. 78) has unstreaked underparts and a white face; Long-eared Owl has distinctive ear tufts when perched.

Quick I.D.: crow-sized; large, round head; yellow eyes encircled by black; vertical streaks on chest, belly and back; long wings; black wrist patches; flight distinctive; sexes similar.

Size: 13–17 in.

Jan Feb Mar Apr May Jun Jul Aug Sept Oct Nov Dec

Rufous Hummingbird

Selasphorus rufus

The Rufous Hummingbird's gentle appearance is misleading: in spring, the male is fiercely aggressive and will chase intruders away in the spirited defense of a food source. Hummingbirds are easily attracted to backyard feeders filled with sweetened water. They are also attracted to red objects, and have been known to closely investigate shirts, lanterns or other backyard objects that are bright red.

Quick I.D.: much smaller than a sparrow.
Male: orange-brown back, tail and flanks; scarlet, scaled throat; green crown.
Female: green back; rufous sides; red spots on throat.
Size: 4 in.

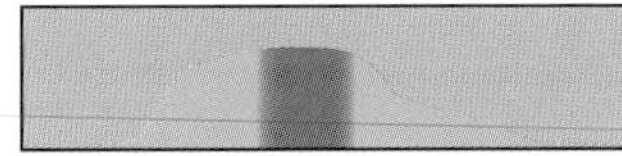

The tiny male performs his towering courtship flight with great speed, which makes it difficult to follow. Performing before a prospective mate, the male's noisy, buzzy flight follows an inverted 'U' pattern. The male climbs high, with his rusty back facing the female, and then from great heights turns and dives quickly toward the female with his crimson throat blazing.

Similar Species: Anna's Hummingbird male has a rose head and throat, but is otherwise green and is larger.

Belted Kingfisher

Ceryle alcyon

Quick I.D.: pigeon-sized; blue-gray back, wings and head; shaggy crest; heavy bill. *Male:* single, blue chest band. *Female:* blue chest band and rust-colored belt.
Size: 12–14 in.

The Belted Kingfisher is found year-round near quiet waters, never far from shore. As the name suggests, kingfishers prey primarily on fish, which they catch with precise headfirst dives. A dead branch extending over fresh- and saltwater will often serve as a perch from which to survey the fish below.

The Belted Kingfisher builds its nest near the end of a long tunnel excavated a few feet into sandy or dirt banks. A rattling call, blue-gray coloration and large crest are the distinctive features of the Belted Kingfisher. With most birds, the males are more colorful, but female Kingfishers are distinguished from males by the presence of a second, rust-colored band across its belly. Although there are many species of kingfisher in the world, the Belted Kingfisher is the only member of its family across most of the United States. The Seattle area is blessed with year-round open water, and Belted Kingfishers can be encountered every day of the year, crashing into calm waters in search of fish.

Similar Species: None.

Red-breasted Sapsucker

Sphyrapicus ruber

With its scarlet hood, the Red-breasted Sapsucker is the most brightly colored of the North American sapsuckers. It can be observed during the summer along the foothills just east of Seattle, and a few birds reliably move into residential areas during the winter months. After a snowstorm or during a period of freezing temperatures, search for its characteristic drill holes in white pines and spruce trees in the Seattle area, and you may be rewarded with a glimpse of this secretive bird.

Sapsuckers drill lines of parallel 'wells' in tree bark. As the wells fill with sap they attract insects, and Red-breasted Sapsuckers make their rounds, drinking the sap and eating the bugs that are trapped in it. Some people find the damaging effect on trees overshadows the bird's resourcefulness, but most healthy trees can withstand a series of sapsucker drillings.

The Red-breasted Sapsucker is one of the easiest woodpeckers to identify by sound. It often meows like a cat, and its territorial drumming sounds like random Morse code.

Similar Species: Other woodpeckers lack the scarlet hood and breast.

Quick I.D.: smaller than a robin; scarlet hood and chest; black and white spots on back and wings; white wing bars; white rump; yellow wash on lower breast to belly; sexes similar.
Size: 7–9 in.

Downy Woodpecker

Picoides pubescens

The Downy Woodpecker is a systematic forager, methodically chipping off dead bark and probing into crevices in search of hidden insects. Because of its small bill, the Downy Woodpecker can find food where larger-billed woodpeckers cannot reach.

As with other woodpeckers, the structure of the Downy Woodpecker's feet and tail help it climb vertically. It can clamp onto a trunk with its two forward-facing and two backward-facing toes, and it can prop its stiff tail against the trunk to steady itself.

The black-and-white Downy Woodpecker is the smallest North American woodpecker, and it is common in wooded ravines and most wooded city parks. It is easily attracted to backyard feeders that offer suet.

Similar Species: Hairy Woodpecker is larger, and it has a longer bill and clean white outer tail feathers.

Quick I.D.: slightly larger than a sparrow; black-and-white wings and back; unmarked, white underparts; short, stubby bill; white outer tail feather is spotted black.
Male: red patch on back of head.
Female: no red patch.
Size: 6–7 in.

Northern Flicker
Colaptes auratus

Walkers strolling through Montlake Fill may be surprised by a woodpecker flushing from the ground before them. As the Northern Flicker beats a hasty retreat, it reveals an unmistakable white rump and red wing linings. It is the least arboreal of our woodpeckers, and it spends more time feeding on the ground than other woodpeckers. Often, it is only when the Northern Flicker is around its nest cavity in a tree that it truly behaves like other woodpeckers: clinging, rattling and drumming.

The Northern Flicker can easily be seen all year, and it occasionally visits backyard feeders when snow blankets the ground. When the ground is free of snow, the Northern Flicker (and other birds) squish ants and then preen themselves with the remains. Ants contain concentrations of formic acid, which is believed to kill small parasites living on the flicker's skin and in its feathers.

Similar Species: Other woodpeckers, Varied Thrush (p. 112) and American Robin (p. 111) all lack the white rump and red wing linings.

Quick I.D.: larger than a robin; brown-barred back; spotted underneath; black bib; white rump; long bill.
Red-shafted form: (main form in Washington) red wing and tail linings; brown crown.
Yellow-shafted form: (rare in western Washington) yellow wing and tail linings; gray crown.
Male Red-shafted: red mustache.
Male Yellow-shafted: black mustache.
Female: no mustache.
Size: 11–14 in.

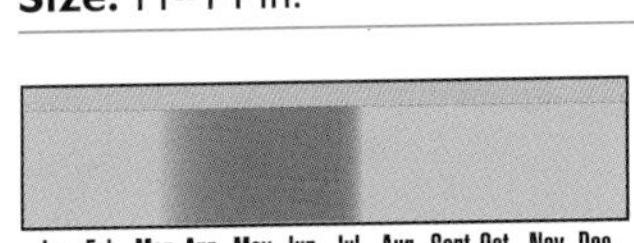

Pileated Woodpecker

Dryocopus pileatus

Although our largest woodpecker is never abundant, all forested areas, even in parks, occasionally ring with its laughing *kik-kik-kik-kik* call. In an unending search for grubs and ants, the Pileated Woodpecker chisels out telltale elliptical cavities with its powerful bill. The distinctive cavities are often the only evidence that a Pileated Woodpecker has been in an area. Many areas of Seattle boast the large, mature trees required by these woodpeckers, which may need up to 1000 acres of mature forest to settle. Occasionally, the swooping, undulating flight of a Pileated Woodpecker can be seen over trees or in forests clearings. Pileated Woodpeckers can occasionally become adapted to suburban areas, and a few resident pairs are often found in Discovery, Seward and Schmitz parks.

There's no real consensus on whether this bird's name is pronounced 'pie-lee-ated' or 'pill-e-ated'; either one is acceptable.

Similar Species: American and Northwestern crows (p. 99) and Common Raven have no white in their wings; other woodpeckers are much smaller.

Quick I.D.: crow-sized; mostly black; white wing linings; flaming red crest.

Male: red mustache; red crest that extends through its forehead.

Female: no mustache; red crest does not extend to forehead.

Size: 16–19 in.

Jan Feb Mar Apr May Jun Jul Aug Sept Oct Nov Dec

Pacific-slope Flycatcher
Empidonax difficilis

Fortunately for birders, the Pacific-slope Flycatcher's song is much more distinctive than its plumage. When you enter any moist woodland in Seattle's urban parks during spring, the Flycatcher's snappy *pawee* is always one of the first sounds you'll hear. This common songbird, formerly grouped with the Cordilleran Flycatcher into a single species—the Western Flycatcher—arrives in Seattle in April and leaves before the end of September.

The genus name *Empidonax* means, quite appropriately, 'lord of the mosquitoes,' and this bird uses the foraging technique made famous by its family. Perched on an exposed limb, the small bird launches after a flying insect and seizes it in mid-air. Holding its catch firmly with its bill, the bird often loops back and lands on the same perch it left moments earlier. This is the art of flycatching, and the Pacific-slope Flycatcher masters this thrilling feeding technique over Seattle.

Similar Species: Willow Flycatcher (p. 90) has a very faint eye-ring, and its song is *fitz-bew*; Hammond's Flycatcher has a dark lower mandible, and its song is *tse-beek*; Western Wood-Pewee has no eye-ring, and it is dusky-colored; Olive-sided Flycatcher has a dark vest, and its song is *quick-three-beers*.

Quick I.D.: sparrow-sized; olive-green upperparts; yellow-green underparts; white eye-ring; two wing bars; dark bill; yellow wash on belly; dark wings and tail; sexes similar.
Size: 5–6 in.

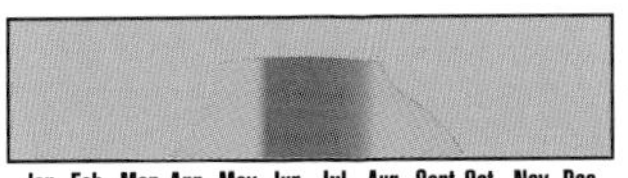

Willow Flycatcher

Empidonax trailii

The empidonax flycatchers (named after their genus) occur throughout North America, and they are famous in birdwatching circles for being hard to identify. Their plumages have slight variations that are obvious only under ideal conditions, but they can best be distinguished from each other by voice and habitat.

Seattle is an exceptionally rich area for flycatchers; the Willow, Pacific-slope and Hammond's flycatchers are frequently seen here. All of their calls are distinctive and simple: the Willow sings a chipper *fitz-bew*, the Hammond's sings a hearty *tse-beek preet*, and the Pacific-slope offers a crisp *pawee.*

The Willow Flycatcher is usually found in brushland and marshes in and around Seattle, and it breeds along the edge of the South Meadow in Discovery Park. A healthy population of this summer resident can be found on Spencer Island in Everett. Pacific-slope Flycatchers are usually found in deciduous forests, while the Hammond's prefers moist conifer woodlands.

Similar Species: Pacific-slope Flycatcher (p. 89), Hammond's Flycatcher and Western Wood-Pewee are all best identified by sound.

Quick I.D.: sparrow-sized; olive-green over-all; faint white eye-ring; two wing bars; dark bill; yellow wash on belly; dark wings and tail; sexes similar.
Size: 5–6 in.

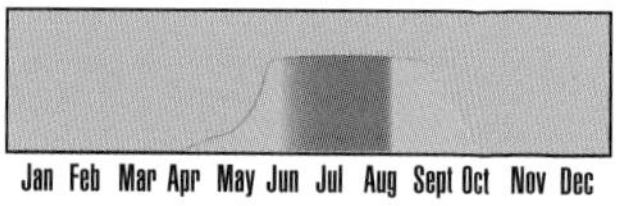

Jan Feb Mar Apr May Jun Jul Aug Sept Oct Nov Dec

Black Swift

Cypseloides niger

One of the positive aspects of gray, wet and cold summer days in Seattle is the Black Swift. Normally a very challenging bird to find in the region, summer low pressure systems force these aerial foragers to feed on flying insects low over the city. During warm, clear days, these masters of flight are infrequently encountered, because they forage over great distances and at such height that they appear as mere specks against the blue sky.

The Black Swift is the largest North American swift, and it also outsizes all swallows in the Seattle area. This swift's flight is distinctive: it alternates long glides with a few leisurely wingbeats. Black Swifts routinely forage great distances from their nests, which are in remote, moist, rocky crevices.

Similar Species: Vaux's Swift (p. 92) and most swallows (pp. 93–96) lack uniformly dark plumage; Purple Martin is rare in Seattle area.

Quick I.D.: larger than a sparrow; dark over-all; long, swept-back wings; short, slightly forked tail; erratic flight; sexes similar.
Size: 7 in.

Jan Feb Mar Apr May Jun Jul Aug Sept Oct Nov Dec

Vaux's Swift

Chaetura vauxi

Quick I.D.: smaller than a sparrow; dark brown overall; long, swept-back wings; squared-off tail; light underparts; darker upperparts; sexes similar.
Size: 4–5 in.

Jan Feb Mar Apr May Jun Jul Aug Sept Oct Nov Dec

Over mixed forests and wetlands, the Vaux's Swift spends most of its waking hours on the wing in vigilant search of flying insects. The wingbeat of swifts appears to alternate and looks uncomfortable, but it doesn't hamper the graceful flight of these aerial masters. While many swifts in the eastern U.S. choose chimneys and other structures in which to nest and roost, the western Vaux's Swift continues to prefer old, decaying trees for its rest area.

Although individual Vaux's Swifts are seen during the spring and summer, this species is most common in Seattle during the fall migration. Beginning in August, Vaux's Swifts are easily found in the company of assorted swallow species, flying above the wetlands and shrublands of Montlake Fill.

Similar Species: Black Swift (p. 91) is larger and darker, and it has a slightly forked tail; Northern Rough-winged Swallow has stubbier wings and light undertail coverts; other swallows are larger and more colorful; Purple Martin is larger and has a slightly forked tail.

Tree Swallow

Tachycineta bicolor

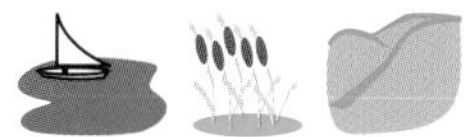

Depending on food availability, Tree Swallows may forage over great distances, darting above open fields and wetlands as they catch flying insects in their bills. These bicolored birds occasionally sweep down to the water surface for a quick drink and bath. In bad weather, Tree Swallows may fly up to 5 miles to distant marshes or lakes to find flying insects.

The Tree Swallow is among the first migrants to arrive in the Seattle area, often beating the onset of spring weather. It returns to Montlake Fill, Juanita Bay on Lake Washington and other freshwater marshes in mid-February to begin its reproductive cycle. It nests in abandoned woodpecker cavities as well as in nest boxes. The cavity is lined with weeds, grasses and long feathers. When the parents leave the eggs for long periods of time, the swallows cover them with the feathers. The females lay and incubate four to six eggs for up to 16 days. Once the birds hatch, the young leave the cavity to begin their aerial lives within three weeks.

Similar Species: Violet-green Swallow (p. 94) has white cheeks and white rump patches; Bank Swallow and Northern Rough-winged Swallow lack the green upperparts.

Quick I.D.: iridescent blue-green plumage; white underparts; no white on cheek; dark rump; small bill; long, pointed wings; shallowly forked tail; small feet; sexes similar.
Size: 5–6 in.

Violet-green Swallow

Tachycineta thalassina

One of the first swallows to return to our area in spring, the Violet-green Swallow soars, dips and dives in forest clearings, fields, marshes and around buildings. These natural flyers spend much of their lives on the wing, and they are frequently seen in the company of look-alike Tree Swallows.

When it is not in the air, the Violet-green Swallow is often encountered in Seattle's neighborhoods, as it regularly nests under the eaves of homes. Should a pair choose to nest in your yard, you can have fun during nest building by tossing feathers in the air: the swallows will grab the feathers from mid-air and use them to line their nest. Unfortunately for the homeowner, the Violet-green Swallow does not linger around the nest site for long after the young have fledged.

Similar Species: Tree Swallow (p. 93) lacks the white face and white saddle patches; most other swallows lack the dark green back and white underparts.

Quick I.D.: sparrow-sized; iridescent green above; white below; white face and saddle patches; short tail; sexes similar.
Size: 5–6 in.

Cliff Swallow
Hirundo pyrrhonota

The Cliff Swallow isn't as widespread in Seattle as the Barn Swallow and the Violet-green Swallow, but where it does occur, you can often encounter it in the hundreds. Cliff Swallows nest under many of the bridges that span our waters, and clouds of them will sometimes whip up on either side of a bridge. They do not restrict their nesting to bridges, however, and colonies are occasionally found under piers, on vacated structures and on dry, rocky cliffs.

If you stop to inspect the undersides of a bridge, you may see hundreds of gourd-shaped mud nests stuck to the pillars and structural beams. The nests are meticulously made from mud, one mouthful at a time. Hundreds of Cliff Swallows busily building nests create a chaotic scene with their constant procession back and forth between nest and mudflat.

Similar Species: Vaux's Swift (p. 92) and Northern Rough-winged Swallow lack the light rump and forehead and the rusty cheeks; Barn Swallow (p. 96) has a deeply forked tail and a dark rump; Tree Swallow (p. 93) has a blue-green back.

Quick I.D.: sparrow-sized; pale forehead; buff rump; dark back with white stripes; gray-brown wings and tail; white underneath; rusty cheeks; dark bib; square tail; sexes similar.
Size: 5–6 in.

Jan Feb Mar Apr May Jun Jul Aug Sept Oct Nov Dec

Barn Swallow

Hirundo rustica

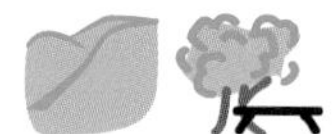

The graceful flight of this bird is a common summer sight. It often forages at low altitudes, so its deeply forked tail is easily observed. The Barn Swallow is actually the only swallow in Seattle to have a 'swallow-tail.' The name 'swallow' originated in Europe, where the Barn Swallow is also common, and where it is simply called the Swallow.

The Barn Swallow builds its cup-shaped mud nests in the eaves of barns and picnic shelters, or in any other structure that provides protection from the rain. Because the Barn Swallow is often closely associated with human structures, it is not uncommon for a nervous parent bird to dive repeatedly at human 'intruders,' encouraging them to retreat.

Similar Species: Cliff Swallow (p. 95) lacks the deeply forked tail, pale forehead and buff rump; Purple Martin has a shorter tail and lacks the russet throat and forehead.

Quick I.D.: larger than a sparrow; deeply forked tail; glossy blue back, wings and tail; chestnut underneath; russet throat and forehead; sexes similar, but female is a bit duller.
Size: 6–8 in.

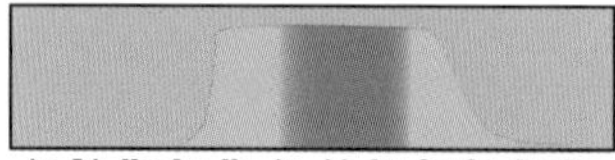

Gray Jay

Perisoreus canadensis

It is impossible to know for certain the reason for the Gray Jay's amicable personality, but it is clear that its friendly behavior is appreciated by humans. Affectionately known as the Whiskey Jack, Canada Jay and Camp Robber (among other names), the bird's list of nicknames is a testament to our appreciation.

The Gray Jay's varied calls can mislead birders, and previously unheard bird songs are often the products of a Gray Jay exercising its diverse vocal repertoire, and not an exotic new bird species.

When most other birds have abandoned the Cascade woods for the winter months, the Gray Jay remains and livens up the short December days. From behind a curtain of fir, a small flock of curious Gray Jays will often arrive to investigate the sounds of an intruder.

Similar Species: Northern Shrike and Northern Mockingbird (uncommon in Seattle) are black and white; Gray Catbird (uncommon in Seattle) has a black cap.

Quick I.D.: larger than a robin; fluffy gray; gray back, wings and tail; pale gray belly and throat; white forehead; long tail; dark nape; dark bill; sexes similar.
Immature: dark gray overall.
Size: 12 in.

Steller's Jay

Cyanocitta stelleri

The Steller's Jay is present throughout the year in coniferous forests west of the Rocky Mountains. With a crest unmatched by any other North American songbird and delicate blue hues sparkling in its plumage, this bird is as striking as it is extroverted and mischievous. It is less known than the familiar Blue Jay to most North Americans, and eastern birdwatchers often visit Seattle to sight them.

Drifting into coastal cities in the late fall and winter, these jays noisily announce their arrival with their *shack-shack-shack* call. The diet of this West Coast jay is diverse: it will eat seeds, dog food and insects, and it will scavenge carcasses.

Steller's Jays travel in loose flocks in August and September, and it is interesting to watch them fly directly to their destination in single-file.

Similar Species: Western Scrub-Jay lacks a crest.

Quick I.D.: larger than a robin; dark crest; blue back, wings and tail; black head; sexes similar.
Size: 11 in.

Jan Feb Mar Apr May Jun Jul Aug Sept Oct Nov Dec

American Crow
Corvus brachyrhynchos

Northwestern Crow
Corvus caurinus

These crows are so similar that they can normally be told apart only by range and voice. Because Seattle lies in the area of overlap of the two species, the confusion is even greater. The American Crow calls with the classic long, descending *caaaw*, while the Northwestern has a hoarser, lower *caar*. The birds themselves refuse to discriminate, and most crows flying around Seattle likely resulted from a certain amount of hybridization.

Crows are capable of solving simple problems, which comes as no surprise to anyone who has watched crows drop shellfish from the air onto rocks, cracking the shells and exposing the meaty flesh. In late summer and fall, when their reproductive duties are completed, crows group together to roost in flocks known as a 'murders.' To experience an amazing winter spectacle, visit Foster Island just before nightfall: there are uncountable numbers of roosting crows.

Similar Species: Common Raven is much larger, and it has a diamond-shaped tail.

Quick I.D.: large crows; black; fan-shaped tail; slim overall; sexes similar. **Size:** 18 in. (American); 17 in. (Northwestern).

Jan Feb Mar Apr May Jun Jul Aug Sept Oct Nov Dec

Black-capped Chickadee

Parus atricapillus

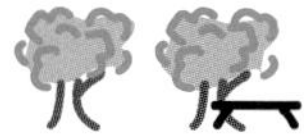

The Black-capped Chickadee is one of the most pleasant birds in urban and forested areas, often seeming to greet walkers along trails. It is a common sight in Seattle and can be found in every park and in most landscaped backyards. Throughout most of the year, chickadees move about in loose flocks, investigating nooks and crannies for food and uttering their delicate *chick-a-dee-dee-dee* calls.

During the spring, Black-capped Chickadees seem strangely absent from city parks and wooded ravines, as they remain inconspicuous while nesting. Once the first fall chill arrives, the woods are once again vibrant with chickadees.

Similar Species: Chestnut-backed Chickadee (p. 101) has a chestnut back; Mountain Chickadee (rare in Seattle) occurs in the mountains, and it has a white eyebrow.

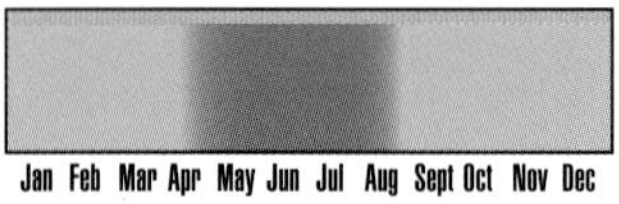

Jan Feb Mar Apr May Jun Jul Aug Sept Oct Nov Dec

Quick I.D.: smaller than a sparrow; black cap and bib; white cheek; grayish back, wings and tail; light underneath; sexes similar.
Size: 5 in.

Chestnut-backed Chickadee

Parus rufescens

This species' greatest abundance is along the Pacific coast in old forests dominated by Sitka spruce. The vivid Chestnut-backed Chickadee is very common on offshore islands, but it is also frequently encountered in Seattle's Discovery and Schmitz parks, and in shrubby backyards. Even before this bird is seen, its *kisssadee* call separates it from its more visible black-capped kin.

These chickadees prefer moist coniferous forests, where they are year-round residents, but they will also visit backyard feeders in well-wooded neighborhoods. Small bands of birds flitting in bushes are likely to be composed of a few Chestnut-backed Chickadees in the company of Golden-crowned Kinglets.

Similar Species: Black-capped Chickadee (p. 100) lacks the chestnut back.

Quick I.D.: smaller than a sparrow; black bib; brown cap; chestnut back; white cheek; grayish wings and tail; light underparts; faint chestnut flanks; sexes similar.
Size: 5 in.

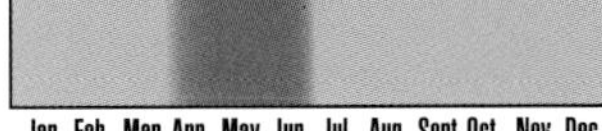

Bushtit

Psaltriparus minimus

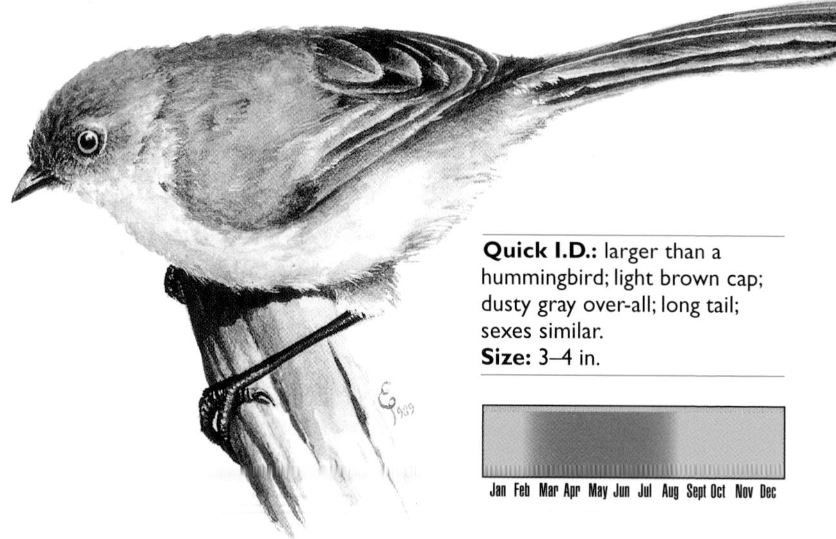

Quick I.D.: larger than a hummingbird; light brown cap; dusty gray over-all; long tail; sexes similar.
Size: 3–4 in.

The character of the home reflects the quality of the occupant, and the tiny gray Bushtit sets a fine example. The architecture of its nest is worth a close look. The intricate weaving of fine fibers, spiderwebs, grasses, mosses and lichens results in what you might mistake for an old gray sock hanging from a brushy shrub.

Their gray-brown bodies are nondescript, but Bushtits are easy to identify because of their behavior: they tend to hang in every position while foraging. Surprisingly tiny, these tufts of continually moving feathers travel in loose flocks, appearing from dense tangles and bushes in all corners of the city. During the winter, they frequently visit backyard feeding stations, and they are very fond of suet. Bushtits often boldly approach close enough to make binoculars unnecessary.

Similar Species: Black-capped Chickadee (p. 100) is larger and has a black bib and cap; all other birds (except hummingbirds) are larger.

Red-breasted Nuthatch

Sitta canadensis

This common year-round resident of coniferous and mixedwood forests has a precarious foraging habit. Unlike other birds, which forage moving up tree trunks or branches, the Red-breasted Nuthatch moves down trunks headfirst. By moving down the tree, it is able to find seeds and insects that have been overlooked by woodpeckers and other bark gleaners. A Red-breasted Nuthatch will occasionally stop with its head held out at a right angle to the trunk.

Birdfeeders in older communities adjacent to mature forests often attract Red-breasted Nuthatches throughout the year. As spring arrives, their distinctive, nasal *yank-yank-yank* call is heard increasingly at the university campus, at Discovery and Seward parks, and in wooded backyards.

Similar Species: White-breasted Nuthatch has a white breast; Downy Woodpecker (p. 86) is black and white.

Quick I.D.: smaller than a sparrow.
Male: red breast; black eyeline; white eyebrow; black cap; steel-blue back, wings and tail; short tail.
Female: similar, but with a gray cap.
Size: 4–5 in.

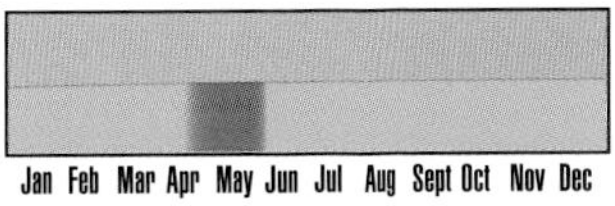

Jan Feb Mar Apr May Jun Jul Aug Sept Oct Nov Dec

Brown Creeper

Certhia americana

The Brown Creeper may be the most inconspicuous bird in North America. Although widespread in forested parks, such as Discovery, Seward and Schmitz, this year-round resident often goes unnoticed until a flake of bark seems to come alive. With short, purposeful, vertical hops, the Brown Creeper spirals up the rugged trunks, constantly probing the tree's wrinkled skin for hidden insect treasures.

When the spiral has reached the upper branches, the tiny bird floats down to the base of a neighboring tree to resume its foraging ascent. Only during these brief flights is the Brown Creeper easily noticed, as even their thin, faint, high-pitched *trees trees trees see the trees* whistle is too high for many birders to hear—it rarely reveals this master of concealment.

Similar Species: Woodpeckers and nuthatches are more colorful.

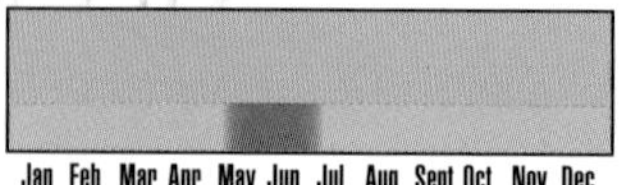

Quick I.D.: smaller than a sparrow; brown back streaked with white; white breast; rusty rump; downcurved bill; long tail; sexes similar.
Size: 5 in.

Bewick's Wren
Thryomanes bewickii

This is the most common backyard wren in Seattle, especially in shrubby areas, and it prefers the undergrowth of our parks and the ornamental shrubs in our yards. The Bewick's Wren's range follows the Pacific coast from the southwestern states to just north of Seattle.

The mission in this wren's life appears to involve the investigation of all suspicious noises, which makes this bird an easy one to attract. These year-round singers are always more abundant than they seem to be, and they frequently nest in backyard nest boxes, natural cavities, wood piles, sheds and garages. Their easily identifiable songs seem individualized, as though each male has added his own twist. Learning the tone and quality of the Bewick's Wren's song is the best way to find this bird.

Similar Species: Winter Wren (p. 106) and House Wren both lack the white eyebrow, and they have shorter tails.

Quick I.D.: smaller than a sparrow; long, brown tail is often cocked up; white eyebrow; light throat and breast; bill slightly downcurved; tail longer than legs; sexes similar.
Size: 5–5½ in.

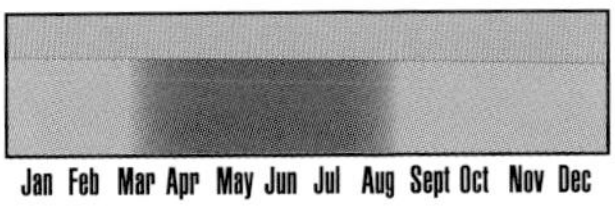

Jan Feb Mar Apr May Jun Jul Aug Sept Oct Nov Dec

Winter Wren

Troglodytes troglodytes

This common bird of suburbs, parks and woodlands sings as though its lungs are bottomless. The song of the Winter Wren is distinguished by its melodious tone and by its endurance. Although far smaller than a sparrow, the Winter Wren offers an unending song of high, tinkling warbles all in one breath.

As spring arrives, the Winter Wren treats coastal residents to a few weeks of wonderful warbles; then it channels its energy into the task of reproduction. By following the song to its source, you may observe a Winter Wren in coastal woodlands, skulking beneath the dense understorey. Like all wrens, this year-round resident frequently carries its short tail cocked straight up.

Similar Species: Bewick's Wren (p. 105) has a white eyebrow and a much longer tail; House Wren has a much longer tail.

Quick I.D.: smaller than a sparrow; brown over-all; cocked-up short tail; sexes similar.
Size: 4 in.

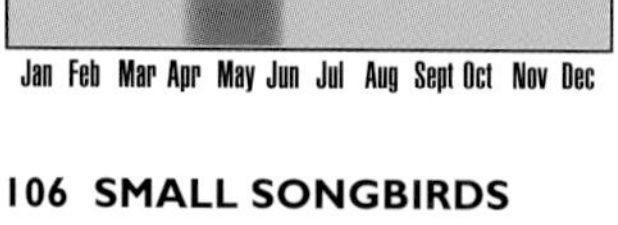

Jan Feb Mar Apr May Jun Jul Aug Sept Oct Nov Dec

Marsh Wren

Cistothorus palustris

This energetic little bird usually lives in cattail marshes and dense, wet meadows bordered by willows. Although it usually sings in the deep vegetation, its distinctive voice is one of the characteristic sounds of our freshwater wetlands. The song has the repetitive quality of an old sewing machine. Once you learn the rhythm, you will hear it whenever you visit freshwater wetlands. In early spring, Montlake Fill and outlying marshes ring with the dynamic call of this reclusive bird.

A typical sighting of a Marsh Wren is spotting a brown blur moving noisily about within shoreline tangles. Although the wren may be less than three yards from the observer, its cryptic habits and appearance are effective camouflage. Patient observers may be rewarded with a brief glimpse of a Marsh Wren perching high atop a cattail reed as it quickly evaluates its territory.

Similar Species: Winter (p. 106), Bewick's (p. 105) and House wrens all have unstreaked backs and generally avoid wetlands.

Quick I.D.: smaller than a sparrow; brown over-all; white streaking on back; white eyeline; light throat and breast; cocked-up tail; sexes similar.
Size: 4–5½ in.

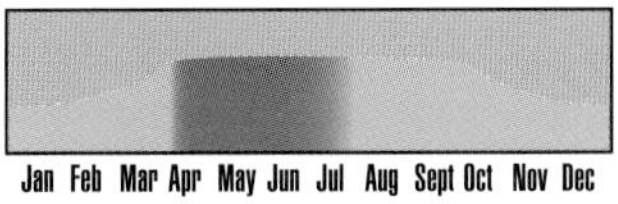

Jan Feb Mar Apr May Jun Jul Aug Sept Oct Nov Dec

Golden-crowned Kinglet

Regulus satrapa

The high-pitched, tinkling voice of the Golden-crowned Kinglet is as familiar as the sweet smell of cedar and fir in coniferous forests. During the winter, the tall conifer canopies in Seattle's parks and older communities are alive with the sound of the Golden-crowned Kinglet's faint, high-pitched, accelerating *tsee-tsee-tsee-tsee, why do you shilly-shally.* A birdwatcher with a keen ear, patience and the willingness to draw down the smallest North American songbird with 'squeaks' and 'pishes' will encounter kinglets on many outdoor trips. The flock will circle about a noise, using branches as swings and trapezes, flashing their regal crowns and repeatedly flicking their wings.

Similar Species: Ruby-crowned Kinglet (p. 109) lacks the black outline to the crown; warblers (pp. 114–20) are generally more colorful or lack the golden crown, and they do not habitually flick their wings.

Jan Feb Mar Apr May Jun Jul Aug Sept Oct Nov Dec

Quick I.D.: smaller than a sparrow; plump; dark olive; white wing bars; dark tail and wings; white eyebrow.
Male: fiery orange crown bordered by black.
Female: lemon-yellow crown bordered by black.
Size: 4 in.

Ruby-crowned Kinglet

Regulus calendula

These kinglets are common winter visitors to Seattle's parks and backyards, especially amongst coniferous trees. They arrive in September and flit continuously through our shrubs until April. Kinglets always appear nervous, with their tails and wings flicking non-stop as they hop from branch to branch in search of grubs and insect eggs.

The Ruby-crowned Kinglet is similar to the Golden-crowned Kinglet in size, habits and coloration, but it has a hidden ruby crown. 'Rubies' are heard far more often then they are seen, especially prior to their spring departure in February through April. Their distinctive song starts like a motor chugging to life, and then the kinglets fire off a series of loud, rising *chewy-chewy-chewy-chewy*. The final phrases are often the only recognizable part of the song.

Similar Species: Golden-crowned Kinglet (p. 108) has a black outline to the crown; Hutton's Vireo (p. 113) is larger and stouter, and it has a stubby bill; Orange-crowned Warbler (p. 114) lacks wing bars.

Quick I.D.: smaller than a sparrow; plump; dark olive; white wing bars; dark tail and wings; incomplete eye-ring.
Male: red crown (infrequently seen).
Female: lacks the red crown.
Size: 4 in.

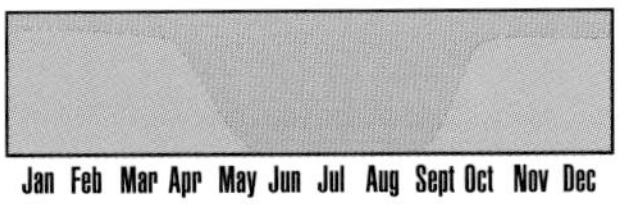

Jan Feb Mar Apr May Jun Jul Aug Sept Oct Nov Dec

Swainson's Thrush

Catharus ustulatus

Beauty in forest birds is often gauged by sound, not appearance. Given this criterion, the Swainson's Thrush is certainly one of the most enchanting birds to inhabit Seattle-area riparian cottonwood forests. Swainson's Thrushes are heard but rarely seen during their summer stay, and they reveal themselves to birders mainly when they flock together in preparation for their southern migration.

The song of the Swainson's Thrush lifts the soul with each note, and it leaves a fortunate listener breathless at its conclusion. The inspiring song is frequently heard in early spring mornings along the Snoqualmie River valley, but the Swainson's Thrush's song is most appreciated at dusk, because this thrush is routinely the last of the daytime singers to be silenced by the night; it alone offers an emotional melody to the darkening forest.

Similar Species: Hermit Thrush has a reddish rump and tail, and golden cheeks, and it often flicks its wings nervously.

Quick I.D.: smaller than a robin; bold white eye-ring; golden cheeks; lightly spotted throat and breast; white belly and undertail coverts; olive-gray flanks; light underparts; sexes similar.
Size: 7 in.

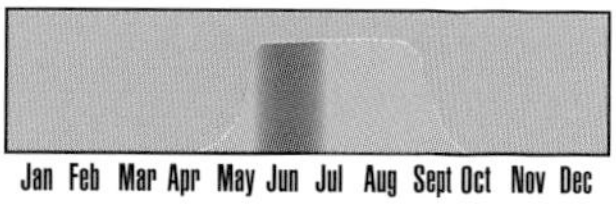

Jan Feb Mar Apr May Jun Jul Aug Sept Oct Nov Dec

American Robin

Turdus migratorius

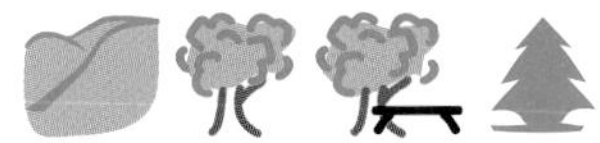

The American Robin's close relationship with urban areas has allowed many residents an insight into a bird's life. A robin dashing around a yard in search of worms or ripe berries is as familiar to many people as its three-part *cheerily-cheery up-cheerio* song. Robins also make up part of the emotional landscape of communities as their cheery song, their spotted young and occasionally even their deaths are experiences shared by their human neighbors.

American Robins appear to be year-round residents in Seattle, but the bird dashing on your lawn in June may not be the same bird that shivers in February. Unnoticed by most Northwest residents, the neighborhood robins take seasonal shifts; some arrive from the north and east when others depart for southern climes.

Similar Species: Varied Thrush (p. 112) has a black mask and a black breast band; immature robins can be confused with other thrushes, but robins always have at least a hint of red in the breast.

Quick I.D.: smaller than a jay; dark head, back and tail; yellow bill; striped throat; white undertail coverts.
Male: brick-red breast; darker hood.
Female: slightly more orange breast; lighter hood.
Size: 9–11 in.

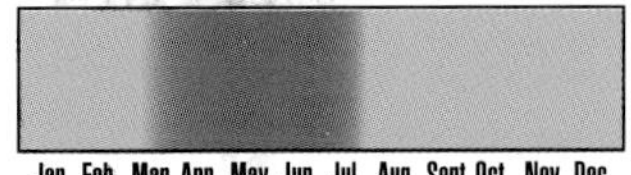

Varied Thrush

Ixoreus naevius

The eerie voice of the Varied Thrush is unlike any other sound in nature. Western residents alone are blessed by the long steam-whistle notes, delivered in well-spaced alternating pitches, that open and close cool, damp spring days.

When October's chill envelops the coastal ranges, many Varied Thrushes move down the slopes to settle in Seattle's urban parks and older communities for the winter. At this time, they grace the forests of Seward and Discovery parks, where they shy away from the mixed-bird flocks that tumble from bush to bush. When the coolest winter days have passed, most Varied Thrushes turn Seattle over to southern migrants and return to the dense woodlands to breed.

Similar Species: American Robin (p. 111) lacks the chest band and mask.

Quick I.D.: robin-sized.
Male: orange underparts; black chest band; black mask; blue-gray back; orange eyebrow; orange wing bars.
Female: colors less intense.
Size: 10 in.

Hutton's Vireo

Vireo huttoni

Quick I.D.: smaller than a sparrow; gray-green upperparts; stout bill; incomplete eye-ring; white wing bars; sexes similar.
Size: 5 in.

In early spring the Hutton's Vireo often sings throughout the day in never-ending triplets. The song is an oscillating *zuwee zu-woo zeeoo*, with the phrases finishing on an upbeat.

It is a year-round resident of Seattle's thickets, but it is never so common that it fails to challenge the birdwatching community. This vireo closely resembles kinglets, a few warblers and other vireos. Persistent and patient birders who wants to see a Hutton's Vireo will succeed if they scrutinize the forests of Discovery, MacDonald and Seward parks.

Similar Species: Orange-crowned Warbler (p. 114) and Warbling Vireo both lack wing bars; Ruby-crowned Kinglet (p. 109) is smaller and has a slimmer bill.

Orange-crowned Warbler

Vermivora celata

Jan Feb Mar Apr May Jun Jul Aug Sept Oct Nov Dec

Quick I.D.: smaller than a sparrow; dusky yellow underparts; darker upperparts; faint orange crown (rarely seen); sexes similar.
Size: 4–5 in.

The tinkling trill of this migrant is far more distinct than its plumage. This bird's species name, *celata*, means 'to conceal in,' and it refers to this warbler's infrequently seen orange crown, but it could just as easily refer to its unmarked dress.

The Orange-crowned Warbler is very common in Seattle from mid-April through August. It nests and feeds in shrubby thickets in city parks, undeveloped lands, and occasionally in forested backyards, where bushes echo with its descending trill.

Similar Species: Hutton's Vireo (p. 113), Yellow Warbler (p. 115) and Wilson's Warbler all have distinctive field marks.

Yellow Warbler

Dendroica petechia

The Yellow Warbler is common in shrublands and in groves of birch, willow and cottonwood. From mid-May through August, this brilliantly colored warbler is easily found in appropriate habitat at Montlake Fill and Foster Island.

During our winters, Yellow Warblers migrate to the tropics, spending September to April in Mexico and South America. The Yellow Warbler's courtship song is a lively *sweet-sweet-sweet I'm so-so sweet.* As one of the most distinctive songs, it is easily recognized in early May despite its eight-month absence. In true warbler fashion, the summertime activities of the Yellow Warbler are energetic and inquisitive, flitting from branch to branch in search of juicy caterpillars, aphids and beetles.

Similar Species: Wilson's Warbler (p. 120) has a small black cap; Orange-crowned Warbler (p. 114) lacks the red breast streaks.

Quick I.D.: smaller than a sparrow; yellow over-all; darker back, wings and tail; dark eye and bill.
Male: fine red streaking on breast.
Female: lacks red streaking.
Size: 4–5 in.

Jan Feb Mar Apr May Jun Jul Aug Sept Oct Nov Dec

Yellow-rumped Warbler

Dendroica coronata

The Yellow-rumped Warbler is the Cadillac of birds—it has all the extras (wing bars, crown, breast streaks, colored rump, etc.). The western race of the Yellow-rumped Warbler has a glorious yellow throat and was formerly called the Audubon's Warbler, distinguishing it from the white-throated eastern form, which was known as the Myrtle Warbler.

Ironically, although the western race bore the name of one of the greatest ornithologists, it was one of the few birds that Audubon failed to meet. Although it no longer officially holds the Audubon title, many western birders continue to refer to this spry bird by its former name, affirming its western roots. At times during the spring and fall migrations, the Yellow-rumped Warbler is abundant throughout the Seattle area; during the summer this bird is noticeably less common.

Similar Species: Townsend's Warbler (p. 118) and Black-throated Gray Warbler (p. 117) both lack the combination of a yellow rump and whitish underparts; eastern Yellow-rumped Warbler (Myrtle Warbler) has a white throat and occurs occasionally during the spring/fall migration.

Quick I.D.: sparrow-sized; blue-black back, tail and wings; yellow rump, shoulder patches and crown; yellow throat; white wing bars; dark chest band; white belly; dark cheek.
Male: bright colors.
Female: less intense colors.
Size: 6 in.

Jan Feb Mar Apr May Jun Jul Aug Sept Oct Nov Dec

Black-throated Gray Warbler

Dendroica nigrescens

Quick I.D.: smaller than a sparrow; white and black face; black throat; blue-gray back; dark wings and tail; white wing bars; white underparts.
Male: larger black bib and crown.
Female: grayish crown; white throat.
Size: 4–5 in.

The Black-throated Gray Warbler is a common summer breeder in Seattle's riverside deciduous forests, though it also can be found in evergreen woodlands. Its spunky *weezy weezy weezy weezy-wheet* song closely resembles those of its close relatives, the Townsend's and Hermit warblers, which both have considerably more yellow in their plumage. These insect eaters are highly migratory, spending most of the fall through late winter in Mexico and South America. Search out the *weezy* whine in your backyard trees or the trailside trees in city parks to experience this western specialty.

Similar Species: Townsend's Warbler (p. 118) has yellow on its face and belly; Black-capped Chickadee (p. 100) has an all-white face.

Townsend's Warbler

Dendroica townsendi

The Townsend's Warbler lives high up in trees in the Pacific Northwest. Its bold colors, flitting habits and unmistakable *weezy weezy weezy weezy tweee* song help to distinguish it from other warblers.

Many species of warbler can coexist in our coniferous forests because they partition the food supplies by foraging exclusively in certain areas of the trees. The Townsend's Warbler breeds at higher elevations (above 2000 feet) in the Cascades and Olympics, but they are easily found in the lowlands around Seattle during spring and fall migration.

Although a few Townsend's Warblers overwinter in Seattle, flocking together with chickadees and nuthatches, most flood into the crowns of our conifers in May, adding a splash of color and sound to the lively spring scene.

Similar Species: Black-throated Gray Warbler (p. 117) lacks the yellow plumage; Hermit Warbler (uncommon in Seattle) lacks the black cheek patch.

Quick I.D.: smaller than a sparrow; black throat; yellow face; dark cheek patch; olive back; dark wings and tail; white wing bars. *Male:* larger black bib.
Size: 5 in.

Common Yellowthroat

Geothlypis trichas

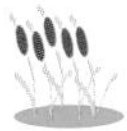

Males of this energetic warbler of the wetlands are easily identified by their black mask or by their oscillating *witchety-witchety-witchety* song. The Common Yellowthroat reaches its highest abundance in Seattle along the wetlands brambles and cattails of Montlake Fill and on Spencer Island, but it can be seen and heard along the vegetation bordering many freshwater bodies.

Female yellowthroats are rarely seen because they keep their nests deep within the thick vegetation surrounding marshes. The Common Yellowthroat's nests are often parasitized by Brown-headed Cowbirds. Since cowbirds are principally birds of the open country, they commonly target the nests of birds that do not nest in deep forests, such as Common Yellowthroats, Yellow Warblers, Red-eyed Vireos and Song Sparrows.

Similar Species: Male is distinct; female is similar to female Nashville Warbler (rare in Seattle), but the female yellowthroat has orange legs.

Quick I.D.: smaller than a sparrow; yellow underparts; olive back; orange legs.
Male: black mask and forehead with white border.
Female: no black mask.
Size: 4 1/2–5 1/2 in.

Wilson's Warbler

Wilsonia pusilla

The hearty chatter of the Wilson's Warbler reveals the presence of this small, colorful bird. It feeds energetically on caterpillars and other insects in branches that are low to the ground, often near water. Often flitting to within a branch of onlookers, the energetic warbler bounces from one perch to another like an overwound wind-up toy.

This warbler was named for Alexander Wilson, the father of American ornithology. During spring and fall migration, Wilson Warblers can be found almost anywhere in Seattle including well-planted backyards. During the nesting season, however, they become far more discriminating and secretive, as they cautiously conceal their nest sites.

Similar Species: Yellow Warbler (p. 115) has a steaked breast, and it lacks the black cap; Orange-crowned Warbler (p. 114) has greener plumage, and it lacks the black cap.

Jan Feb Mar Apr May Jun Jul Aug Sept Oct Nov Dec

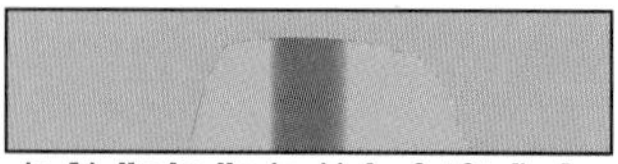

Quick I.D.: smaller than a sparrow; lemon-yellow underparts; olive to dark green upperparts.
Male: black cap.
Female: no black cap.
Size: 5 in.

Western Tanager

Piranga ludoviciana

Quick I.D.: smaller than a robin.
Male: yellow body with contrasting black wings and tail; red on head.
Female and *Non-breeding Male:* olive-yellow over-all.
Size: 7 in.

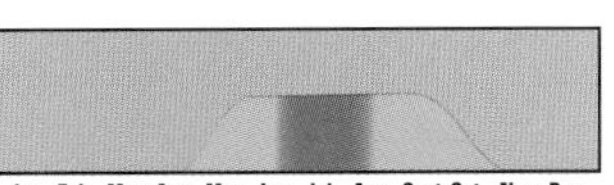

Arriving in Seattle woodlands in mid-May, the male Western Tanager, which is splashed with red, yellow and black, sings robin-like songs high in the forest canopy. Despite the male tanager's colorful attire, it often remains inconspicuous on its breeding grounds. Tracing the easily learned song and *pit-a-tik* call to its source is the best way to discover this tropically dressed bird, which frequently remains on the same treetop perch for long periods of time. This is one of Seattle's most beautiful birds, and every possible encounter with it should be fully enjoyed.

Similar Species: Black-headed Grosbeak (p. 140) and Bullock's Oriole (p. 135) both lack the yellow body plumage.

European Starling
Sturnus vulgaris

In 1945, 55 years after their intentional release in New York's Central Park, European Starlings began to establish themselves in Washington State. Less than a decade later, flocks of 5000 were being reported at Lake Washington. Today, European Starlings are one of the most common birds throughout Seattle. Their presence is highlighted by astonishing numbers roosting communally during the winter months.

Unfortunately, the expansion of starlings has come at the expense of many native birds in the Seattle area, including the Purple Martin and the Western Bluebird, which are unable to defend their nest cavities against the aggressive starling. While not all birdwatchers are pleased with the presence of this foreigner to Seattle, starlings have become a permanent fixture in the bird community. If residents are unable to find joy in this bird's mimicry and flocking, they may take some comfort from the fact that starlings now provide a reliable and stable food source for woodland hawks and the Peregrine Falcon.

Similar Species: All blackbirds have a long tail and a black bill; Purple Martin has a short bill.

Jan Feb Mar Apr May Jun Jul Aug Sept Oct Nov Dec

Quick I.D.: smaller than a robin; short tail; sexes similar.
Breeding: dark, glossy plumage; long, yellow bill.
Non-breeding: dark bill; spotty plumage.
Immature: brown upperparts; gray-brown underparts; brown bill.
Size: 9 in.

Cedar Waxwing

Bombycilla cedrorum

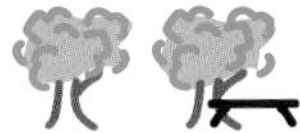

A faint, high-pitched trill is often your first clue that waxwings are around. Search the treetops to see these cinnamon-crested birds as they dart out in quick bursts, snacking on flying insects. Cedar Waxwings are found in many habitats, from the forests of Discovery, Seward and Lincoln's parks to the open areas over Green Lake and the Ballard Locks.

Cedar Waxwings are most often seen in large flocks in late summer, when they congregate on fruit trees and quickly eat all the berries. Some people remember these visits not only for the birds' beauty, but because occasionally the fermentation of the fruit renders the flock flightless from intoxication. During harsh winters, Seattle is occasionally visited by the Bohemian Waxwing, a large cousin of the Cedar Waxwing.

Similar Species: Bohemian Waxwing is slightly larger, and it has chestnut undertail coverts and red and yellow droplets on the wingtips.

Quick I.D.: smaller than a robin; fine, pale brown plumage; small crest; black mask; yellow belly wash; yellow-tipped tail; light undertail coverts; shiny red (waxy-looking) droplets on wingtips; sexes similar.
Size: 8 in.

Jan Feb Mar Apr May Jun Jul Aug Sept Oct Nov Dec

Spotted Towhee

Pipilo maculatus

This large, colorful sparrow is most often heard scratching away leaves and debris in the dense understorey before it is seen. It is a common year-round resident in many of Seattle's parks and shrubby backyards. Deep in the shadows of shrubs, the Spotted Towhee's sharp *t'wee* identifies this secretive sparrow.

To best observe this bird, which was formerly grouped with the Eastern Towhee (and together known as the Rufous-sided Towhee), learn a few birding tricks. Squeaking and pishing are irresistible for towhees, which will quickly pop out from the cover to investigate the curious noise.

Similar Species: American Robin (p. 111) is larger and lacks white on its chest; Dark-eyed Junco (p. 130) is smaller and has white outer tail feathers.

Jan Feb Mar Apr May Jun Jul Aug Sept Oct Nov Dec

Quick I.D.: smaller than a robin; black head; rufous-colored flanks; spotted back; white outer tail feathers and underparts; red eyes.
Male: black head, breast and upperparts.
Female: reddish-brown head, breast and upperparts.
Size: 9 in.

Savannah Sparrow

Passerculus sandwichensis

The Savannah Sparrow is one of the most widespread birds in North America. Open country in Seattle, open areas along the coast, and grasslands in lowland areas all host this common sparrow. It breeds in fields of weedy annuals and grasses at Montlake Fill and at Discovery and Magnuson parks.

The Savannah Sparrow resorts to flight only as a last alternative: it prefers to run swiftly and inconspicuously through long grass, and it is most often seen darting across roads and open fields. Its dull brown plumage and streaked breast conceal it perfectly in the long grasses of meadows, farms and roadsides. The Savannah Sparrow's distinctive buzzy trill—*tea-tea-tea-teeea today*—and the yellow patch in front of each eye are the best ways to distinguish it from the many other grassland sparrows.

Similar Species: Lincoln's Sparrow has a buffy head and breast and a wren-like song.

Quick I.D.: small sparrow; streaked underparts and upperparts; mottled brown above; dark cheek; no white outer tail feathers; many have yellow lores; sexes similar.
Size: 5 in.

Jan Feb Mar Apr May Jun Jul Aug Sept Oct Nov Dec

Fox Sparrow
Passerella iliaca

The Fox Sparrow is a year-round resident in Seattle's thickets and brambles, although it is most common from October through April. Like many other sparrows that winter in this habitat, the Fox Sparrow is appreciated for its voice more than for its plumage. Although the subtlety of the Fox Sparrow's plumage is beautiful, its voice overshadows its appearance. During late winter, sit and wait near tangles and brush piles in Seattle's parks, and listen as the Fox Sparrow repeatedly belts out its distinctive musical question: *all I have is what's here dear, will-you-will-you take-it?*

Similar Species: Song Sparrow (p. 128) has a different song and a much lighter color; Lincoln's Sparrow has weaker breast streaks; Swainson's Thrush (p. 110) has a pale eye-ring and olive upperparts.

Quick I.D.: large sparrow; heavy breast streaks form dark chest; brown plumage; very dark over-all; sexes similar.
Size: 6½–7 in.

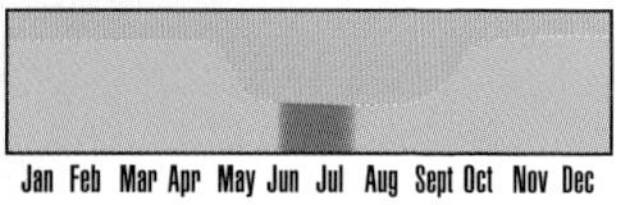

Jan Feb Mar Apr May Jun Jul Aug Sept Oct Nov Dec

Song Sparrow

Melospiza melodia

Quick I.D.: large sparrow; heavy breast streaks form central chest spot; brown-red plumage; striped head; white trailing down from bill; sexes similar.
Size: 6 in.

The Song Sparrow's drab, heavily streaked plumage doesn't prepare you for its symphonic song, which stands among those of the great Seattle songsters in complexity and rhythm: this commonly heard bird seems to be singing *hip-hip-hip hooray boys, the spring is here again.*

This year-round resident is encountered in a wide variety of habitats. Song Sparrows are easily found in all seasons among thickets, blackberry brambles, weedy fields and woodland edges. Although these birds are most easily identified by their grayish streaks while perched, flying birds will characteristically pump their tails.

Similar Species: Fox Sparrow (p. 126) is very heavily streaked and has a different song; Savannah Sparrow (p. 125) and Lincoln's Sparrow have weaker breast streaks.

White-crowned Sparrow

Zonotrichia leucophrys

White-crowned Sparrows are usually seen foraging on the ground or in low shrubs. They normally feed a short distance from thickets and tall grasses, always maintaining a quick escape path into the safety of concealing vegetation. Overwintering White-crowned Sparrows sporadically appear to feed at backyard feeders.

These common year-round residents of the Pacific Northwest represent a distinct subspecies of the White-crowned Sparrow. Seattle's White-crowns tend to have white lores, brown upperparts and gray-brown underparts.

During early spring, these large sparrows are frequently heard singing their utterly distinctive phrase—*I-I-I-I gotto go wee wee wee now*—from the tops of bushes all along the West Coast. White-crowns are very persistent singers, and their songs can be heard well into Seattle's spring nights.

Similar Species: Golden-crowned Sparrow (p. 129) has a golden-yellow crown; White-throated Sparrow (uncommon in Seattle) has yellow lores and a clear white throat.

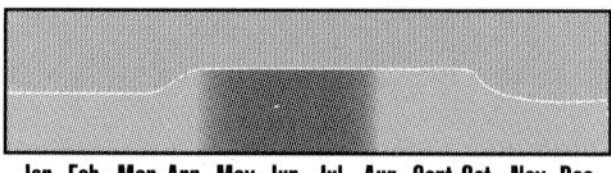

Jan Feb Mar Apr May Jun Jul Aug Sept Oct Nov Dec

Quick I.D.: large sparrow; striped, black-and-white crown; pink bill; unstreaked breast; yellow wing edge; brown upperparts; gray-brown underparts; sexes similar. *Immature:* brown crown; buffy-olive upperparts; faint yellow underparts. **Size:** 5$^1/_2$–7 in.

Golden-crowned Sparrow

Zonotrichia atricapilla

Quick I.D.: large sparrow; golden-yellow crown; thick black eyebrow extending all around head; gray cheek; unstreaked breast; sexes similar.
Immature: light streaking on head; often faint yellow forehead.
Size: 7 in.

The Golden-crowned Sparrow's *oh, dear me!* song can be heard from dense thickets and brush piles across the Northwest during spring migration. This western sparrow is striking, with broad black eyebrows capped in gold. On a crisp October morning, Montlake Fill, Discovery Park and Magnuson Park are some of the best places to watch the Golden-crowned Sparrow fly from bush to bush. During the winter months, many visit backyards, picking up and eating bird seed that has been dropped to the ground from raised feeders.

Similar Species: White-crowned Sparrow (p. 128) and White-throated Sparrow both lack the yellow crown.

Dark-eyed Junco

Junco hyemalis

Quick I.D.: large sparrow; black hood; brown back; pinkish sides; pink bill; white outer tail feathers; white belly; sexes similar.

Size: 5–6½ in.

Jan Feb Mar Apr May Jun Jul Aug Sept Oct Nov Dec

While Americans east of the Rockies do have Dark-eyed Juncos, only West Coast residents have the splashy race with the black hood and tail and the pinkish body, which is sometimes called the Oregon Junco.

The Dark-eyed Junco is a ground dweller, and it is frequently seen as it flushes from the undergrowth along wooded trails in Seattle's parks. The distinctive white outer tail feathers will flash in alarm as it flies down a narrow path before disappearing into a thicket. The junco's distinctive smacking call and its habit of double-scratching at forest litter also help identify it.

While most Dark-eyed Juncos breed away from the city, they are abundant winter visitors in Seattle. They are common guests at birdfeeders, and they usually pick up the scraps that have fallen to the ground.

Similar Species: Spotted Towhee (p. 124) is larger and has white 'flaking' on back; Brown-headed Cowbird (p. 134) lacks the white outer tail feathers.

Red-winged Blackbird

Agelaius phoeniceus

From March through July, no marsh is free from the loud calls and bossy, aggressive nature of the Red-winged Blackbird. A springtime walk around the perimeter of Green Lake or through the brush at Montlake Fill will be accompanied by this blackbird's loud, raspy and persistent *konk-a-reee* or *eat my CHEEEzies* song. The male's bright red shoulders are his most important tool in the strategic and intricate displays he uses to defend his territory from rivals and to attract a mate. In experiments, males whose red shoulders were painted black soon lost their territories to rivals they had previously defeated.

The female's interest lies not in the individual combatants, but in nesting habitat, and a male who can successfully defend a large area of dense cattails will breed with many females. After the females have built their concealed nests and laid their eggs, the male continues his persistent vigil.

Similar Species: Brewer's Blackbird (p. 133) and Brown-headed Cowbird (p. 134) both lack the red shoulder patches.

Quick I.D.: smaller than a robin.
Male: all-black plumage; large red and small yellow patch on each shoulder (yellow not always evident).
Female: brown over-all; heavily streaked; hint of red on shoulder.
Size: 7½–9½ in.

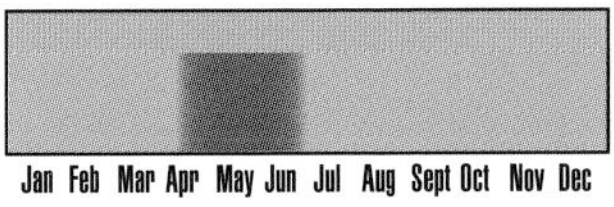

Jan Feb Mar Apr May Jun Jul Aug Sept Oct Nov Dec

Western Meadowlark

Sturnella neglecta

Quick I.D.: robin-sized; mottled brown upperparts; black 'V' on chest; yellow throat and belly; white outer tail feathers; striped head; sexes similar.
Size: 8–10 in.

Jan Feb Mar Apr May Jun Jul Aug Sept Oct Nov Dec

Although a few Western Meadowlarks may breed around Seattle, their occurrence is most notable during the winter months. The fiercely defended summer solitude and territoriality of this open-country bird is abandoned in winter, and flocks of up to 40 meadowlarks can be seen wheeling over open fields, pastures and river deltas, taking off and alighting in unison. The pursuit of Western Meadowlarks is most rewarding in the Kent Valley and the Snoqualmie and Cedar river valleys, from October through March.

The Western Meadowlark is well adapted to wide open spaces: its long legs carry it quickly through the grass, and its mottled color blends with the often drab surroundings. In anticipation of its spring departure, Western Meadowlarks may begin to sing in March, offering up their melodies to the fields in which they wintered.

Similar Species: None.

Brewer's Blackbird

Euphagus cyanocephalus

Quick I.D.: robin-sized; long tail; slim bill.
Male: all-black plumage; slightly iridescent; light yellow eyes.
Female: brown over-all; brown eyes.
Size: 8–10 in.

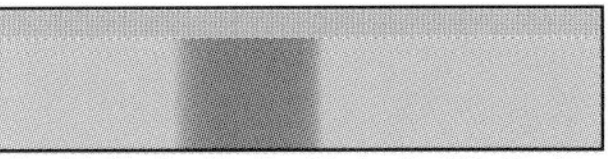

These small blackbirds are common at Green Lake and Alki Point, where they squabble with pigeons and starlings for leftover scraps of food. In the Seattle area, this species is most abundant in rural pastureland, river valleys and along highways, where they are observed strutting confidently in defiance of nearby, rapidly moving vehicles.

Brewer's Blackbirds are bold, and they allow us to easily and intimately observe them. By studying the behavior of several birds within a flock, you can determine the hierarchy of the flock as it is perceived by the birds themselves. Brewer's Blackbird feathers, which superficially appear black, actually show an iridescent quality as reflected rainbows of sunlight move along the feather shafts.

Similar Species: Red-winged Blackbird (p. 131) has a red patch on each wing; male Brown-headed Cowbird (p. 134) has a brown hood; female and immature Brown-headed Cowbirds have a shorter tail and a stout bill.

Brown-headed Cowbird

Molothrus ater

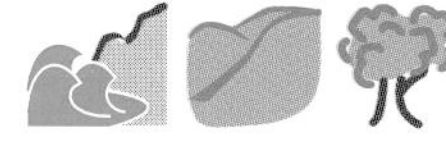

Quick I.D.: smaller than a robin. *Male:* metallic-looking, glossy black plumage; soft brown head; dark eyes. *Female:* brownish gray over-all; dark eye; slight chest streaks.
Size: 6–8 in.

Since it first arrived in the Seattle area in 1954, the Brown-headed Cowbird has firmly established itself within the matrix of the region's bird life. This gregarious bird is very common in city parks during the summer months, and it often forages amidst the driftwood piles at West Point. During the winter, it commonly mixes with other blackbirds in outlying agricultural areas.

The Brown-headed Cowbird is infamous for being a nest parasite—female cowbirds do not incubate their own eggs, but instead lay them in the nests of many songbirds. Cowbird eggs have a short incubation period, and the cowbird chicks often hatch before the host songbird's own chicks. Many songbirds do not recognize that the fast-growing cowbird chick is not one of their own, and they will continue to feed it even after the cowbird chick has grown larger than the songbird. In its efforts to get as much food as possible, a cowbird chick will often squeeze the host's own young out of the nest. The populations of some songbirds have been reduced in part by the activities of the Brown-headed Cowbird, but other songbird species recognize the foreign egg, and they either eject it from their nest or they build a new nest.

Similar Species: Male Brewer's Blackbird (p. 133) has body plumage that is similar to its head color, and it has a yellow eye; female Brewer's Blackbird has a long tail and a thin bill.

Bullock's Oriole
Icterus bullockii

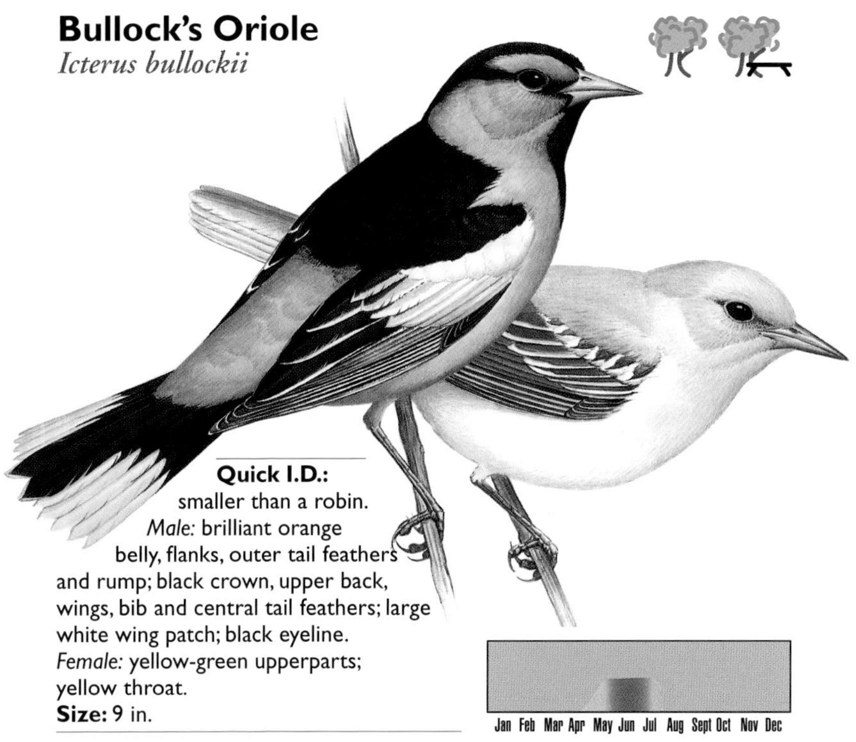

Quick I.D.: smaller than a robin. *Male:* brilliant orange belly, flanks, outer tail feathers and rump; black crown, upper back, wings, bib and central tail feathers; large white wing patch; black eyeline. *Female:* yellow-green upperparts; yellow throat.
Size: 9 in.

Although it is a common summer resident of city parks and wooded valleys, the Bullock's Oriole is seldom seen. Unlike the American Robin, which inhabits the human domain of shrubs and lawns, the Bullock's Oriole nests and feeds in the tallest deciduous trees available. The vacant nest, which is easily seen on bare trees in the fall, is often the only indication that a pair of orioles summered in an area. This bird's hanging, 6-inch-deep, pouch-like nest is deceptively strong. It is principally made by the female, which incubates the four to five eggs for approximately two weeks.

The male Bullock's Oriole's striking, Halloween-like, black-and-orange plumage flashes like embers amidst the dense foliage of the tree-tops, while its slow purposeful *Peter Peter here here Peter Peter* song drips to the forest floor.

From mid-May to mid-July, mature cottonwood forests at Foster Island and Lake Sammamish State Park are the most productive destinations for oriole-starved Seattle-area birdwatchers.

Similar Species: Western Tanager (p. 121) has yellow plumage, a relatively shorter tail and a heavier bill.

Purple Finch

Carpodacus purpureus

Quick I.D. sparrow-sized. *Male:* raspberry head, nape, throat and rump; reddish-brown cheek; streaked back; white undertail coverts. *Female:* brown over-all; streaked underparts; white eyebrow; brown cheek; forked tail.
Size: 6 in.

The annual spring courtship of the Purple Finch may be observed in Seattle's heavily forested parks. The liquid warbling song of the males bubbles through the boughs of conifers. The colorful male also dances around the female while beating his wings quickly, until he gently lifts off the ground.

The Purple Finch is a year-round resident in the Seattle area. It is easily confused with the common House Finch, which is abundant throughout the city. The Purple Finch favors areas of heavy forests, such as Seward, Lincoln and Discovery parks. It is a blessing during winter days, because its raspberry plumage brings a colorful glimmer to backyard feeding stations.

Similar Species: Male House Finch (p. 137) has a darker red breast, a brown cap, a streaked belly and streaked undertail coverts; female Black-headed Grosbeak (p. 140) is larger and has white wing bars.

House Finch

Carpodacus mexicanus

The House Finch is one of the earliest voices to announce the upcoming spring. These common city and country birds sing their melodies from backyards, parks, ivy vines and telephone lines.

During the 1920s and 1930s, these birds, native to the American Southwest, were popular cage birds, and they were sold across the continent as Hollywood Finches. Illegal releases of the caged birds and expansion from their historic range have resulted in two separate distributions in North America that are destined to converge. Seattle's House Finches, now familiar throughout the city, first arrived in 1953.

Similar Species: Male Purple Finch (p. 136) is raspberry-colored and has unstreaked undertail coverts; female Purple Finch has a brown cheek contrasting with a white eyebrow and a mustache stripe.

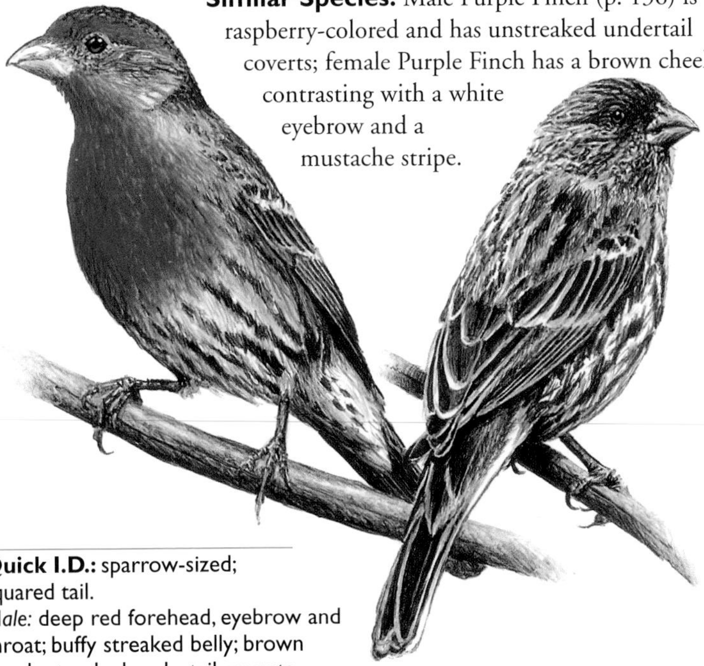

Quick I.D.: sparrow-sized; squared tail.
Male: deep red forehead, eyebrow and throat; buffy streaked belly; brown cheek; streaked undertail coverts.
Female: brown over-all; streaked underparts; brown face; no eyebrow.
Size: 5–5½ in.

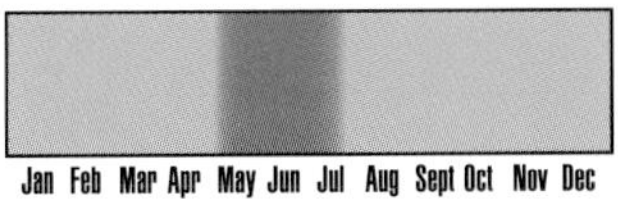

Jan Feb Mar Apr May Jun Jul Aug Sept Oct Nov Dec

Pine Siskin

Carduelis pinus

Quick I.D.: sparrow-sized; lightly streaked underparts; yellow flashes in wings and tail; streaked brown upperparts; sexes similar.
Size: 5 In.

Tight, wheeling flocks of these gregarious birds are frequently heard before they are seen. Their characteristic call—*zzzweeet*—starts off slowly and then climbs to a high-pitched climax. Once you recognize this distinctive call, a flurry of activity in the treetops, showing occasional flashes of yellow, will confirm the presence of Pine Siskins.

The Pine Siskin is a year-round, but unpredictable, resident in Seattle, and in all seasons it can be found in moist conifer stands in most of the larger parks. Occasionally, flocks descend into weedy fields and shrubby areas, where the siskins use their pointed bills to extract the seeds of birch trees, red alder and thistles in the fall.

Similar Species: Song Sparrow (p. 127), Fox Sparrow (p. 126), female finches and female crossbills all lack the yellow wing and tail linings.

American Goldfinch
Carduelis tristis

In the spring, the American Goldfinch swings over fields in its distinctive, undulating flight, and it fills the air with its jubilant *po-ta-to chip!* call. The state bird of Washington is a bright, cheery songbird that is commonly seen during the summer in weedy fields, roadsides and backyards, where it often feeds on thistle seeds. The American Goldfinch delays nesting until June or July to ensure a dependable source of insects, thistles and dandelion seeds to feed its young.

The American Goldfinch is a common backyard bird in the Seattle area, and it can easily be attracted to feeding stations that offer a supply of niger seed. Unfortunately, goldfinches are easily bullied at feeders by larger sparrows and finches. Only goldfinches and Pine Siskins invert for food, however, so a special finch feeder with openings below the perches is ideal for ensuring a steady stream of these 'wild canaries.'

Similar Species: Evening Grosbeak (p. 141) is much larger; Yellow Warbler (p. 115) and Wilson's Warbler (p. 120) do not have black on their forehead or wings.

Quick I.D.: sparrow-sized.
Breeding Male: black forehead, wings and tail; canary-yellow body; wings show white in flight.
Female and *Non-breeding Male:* lack black forehead; yellow-green over-all; black wings and tail.
Size: 4½–5½ in.

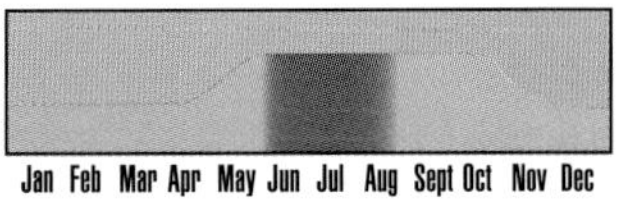

Jan Feb Mar Apr May Jun Jul Aug Sept Oct Nov Dec

Black-headed Grosbeak

Pheucticus melanocephalus

Quick I.D.: smaller than a robin; light-colored, conical bill. *Male:* black head, wings and tail; orange body; white wing patches. *Female:* finely streaked with brown; white eyebrow; light throat.
Size: 7–8½ in.

The male Black-headed Grosbeak has a brilliant voice to match his Halloween plumage, and he flaunts his song in treetop performances. This common songster's boldness does not go unnoticed by the appreciative birding community, which eagerly anticipates the male's annual spring concert to the Snoqualmie River valley and on Spencer Island. The female lacks the formal dress, but she shares her partner's musical talents; whether the nest is tended by the male or female, the developing young are continually introduced into the world of song by the brooding parent.

This neotropical migrant nests in mature deciduous forests, such as those found in parts of Discovery and Lincoln's parks or in less developed urban areas.

Similar Species: Male is distinctive; female is similar to, but generally larger than, female Purple Finch (p. 136) and other sparrows (pp. 125–29).

Evening Grosbeak

Coccothraustes vespertinus

Unlike many North American finches that have extremely variable migratory patterns, the Evening Grosbeak is a regular and predictable spring migrant in Seattle. It is unlikely that the Evening Grosbeak breeds within the city—it usually spends the summer in the forests on the eastern slopes of the Cascades—but it makes a prolonged stopover before continuing up the mountain ranges.

In Ravenna and Discovery parks, Evening Grosbeaks land on budding big leaf maple trees and gorge themselves for several weeks each May. These golden birds are usually heard before they are seen, and their large, gregarious flocks are a special spring treat and a sure sign of the changing seasons.

Similar Species: American Goldfinch (p. 139) is much smaller, and the black on its head is confined to the forehead.

Quick I.D.: smaller than a robin; large, conical bill.
Male: yellow body; dark hood; black tail and wings; bold, white wing patches; yellow eyebrow stripe.
Female: similar to male but lacks bold eyebrow and bright gold body color.
Size: 8 in.

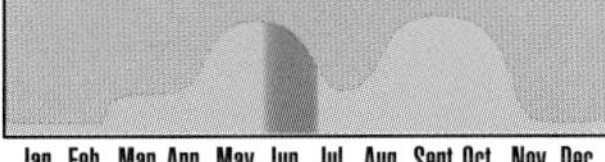

House Sparrow

Passer domesticus

This common backyard bird often confuses novice birdwatchers because females and immatures can be very nondescript. The male is relatively conspicuous—he has a black bib, a gray cap and white lines trailing down from his mouth (as though he has spilled milk on himself)—and he sings a continuous series of *cheep-cheep-cheep.* The best field mark for the female, apart from her pale eyebrows, is that there are no distinctive field marks.

The House Sparrow was introduced to North America in the 1850s to control insects. Although this familiar bird can consume great quantities of insects, the majority of its diet is seeds, and it has become somewhat of a pest. The House Sparrow's aggressive nature usurps several native songbirds from nesting cavities, and its boldness often drives other birds away from backyard feeders. The House Sparrow and the European Starling are now two of the most common birds in cities and on farms, and they are a constant reminder of the negative impact of human introductions on natural systems.

Similar Species: Female sparrows and finches are similar to the female House Sparrow.

Quick I.D.: medium-sized sparrow; brownish-gray belly.
Male: black throat; gray forehead; white jowls; chestnut nape.
Female: plain; pale eyebrow; mottled wings.
Size: $5\frac{1}{2}$–$6\frac{1}{2}$ in.

Jan Feb Mar Apr May Jun Jul Aug Sept Oct Nov Dec

Watching Birds

Identifying your first new bird can be so satisfying that you just might become addicted to birdwatching. Luckily, birdwatching does not have to be expensive. It all hinges on how involved in this hobby you want to get. Setting up a simple backyard feeder is an easy way to get to know the birds sharing your neighborhood, and some people simply find birdwatching a pleasant way to complement a nightly walk with the dog or a morning commute into work.

Many people enjoy going to urban parks and feeding the wild birds that have become accustomed to humans. This activity provides people with intimate contact with urban-dwelling birds, but remember that birdseed, or better yet the birds' natural food items, are much healthier for the birds than bread and crackers. Many ponds in Seattle's parks have signs discouraging such feedings, but the practice persists. As a spokesperson for the animals' health, kindly remind 'bread tossers' of the implications of their actions.

SEASONS OF BIRDWATCHING

Spring

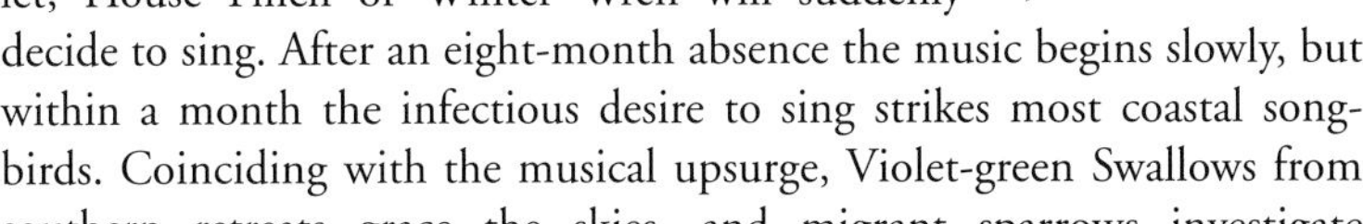

A calendar indicates the arrival of spring around March 21st, but for birdwatchers, the changing season is indicated by migration and bird songs. One brisk morning in February, a Ruby-crowned Kinglet, House Finch or Winter Wren will suddenly decide to sing. After an eight-month absence the music begins slowly, but within a month the infectious desire to sing strikes most coastal songbirds. Coinciding with the musical upsurge, Violet-green Swallows from southern retreats grace the skies, and migrant sparrows investigate brambles and shrubs.

Coastal activities mirror those inland, as overwintering loons, grebes and waterfowl trickle away to their inland breeding grounds. Brant pass through, followed weeks later by clouds of 'wind birds' (sandpipers and plovers). Shorebirds descend in uncountable flocks, coating mudflats and rich shorelines in soul-tickling scenes. Soon the beaches are empty, and forests no longer ring with a multitude of songs. It is time for the serious business of nesting.

Summer

Summertime finds birds busy with their nesting and less likely to put on shows for human observers. Singing gives way to nest-building and incubation. Once the chicks are born, the parents are kept busy feeding the insatiable young.

Summer can be extremely enjoyable for Seattle residents who have set out nest boxes. Watching the birds' reproductive cycles, from breeding to fledging, can provide some memorable experiences. Long, warm days invite us into nature's realm and offer opportunities to visit nearby state and national parks. It is during these excursions that most memorable bird encounters are experienced.

Fall

The fall migration through Seattle is not as focused as that of the spring, but it is not as rushed either, and the fall migration season tends to last months instead of weeks. Geographical features once again funnel birds across the state, with periodic concentrations gathering along the shorelines of Puget Sound. Small flocks are often silent, and they lack the vivid colors of their springtime surge. Fall flocks often include birds of several different species; in spring the birds are most focused on their own species. Migrant species disappear slowly, their numbers gently trickling out with the coming of the cold.

Winter

Far from the desolate landscape that enslaves inland birdwatching communities, Seattle remains a haven for birds in winter. Open water and mild winters attract thousands of waterbirds. Occasional irruptions of finches may descend on backyard feeders to join the more habitual winter jays, juncos and chickadees. Winter is the time for birdfeeders, and a productive yard may reveal a surprising diversity of species. It is also at this time of year that the birdwatcher can arrange field notes, photos and plan upcoming trips for the spring. But take care not to overlook the wintering birds, as their resilience and fortitude are characteristics most enviable on crisp mornings.

BIRDING OPTICS

Most people who are interested in birdwatching will eventually buy a pair of binoculars. They help you identify key bird characteristics, such as plumage and bill color, and they also help you identify other birders! Birdwatchers are a friendly sort, and a chat among birders is all part of the experience.

You'll use your binoculars often, so select a pair that will contribute to the quality of your birdwatching experience—they don't have to be expensive. If you need help deciding which pair would be right for you, talk to other birdwatchers or to someone at your local nature centre. Many models are available, and when shopping for binoculars it's important to keep two things in mind: weight and magnification.

One of the first things you'll notice about binoculars (apart from the price extremes) is that they all have two numbers associated with them (8x40, for example). The first number, which is always the smallest, is the magnification (how large the bird will appear), while the second is the size (in millimeters) of the objective lens (the larger end). It may seem important at first to get the highest magnification possible, but a reasonable magnification of 7x–8x is optimal for all-purpose birding, because it draws you fairly close to most birds without causing too much shaking. Some shaking happens to everyone; to overcome it, rest the binoculars against a support, such as a partner's shoulder or a tree.

The size of the objective lens is really a question of birding conditions and weight. Because wider lenses (40–50 mm) will bring in more light, these are preferred for birding in low-light situations (like before sunrise or after sunset). If these aren't the conditions that you will be pursuing, a light pair that has an objective lens diameter of less than 30 mm may be the right choice. Because binoculars tend to become heavy after hanging around your neck all day, the compact models are becoming increasingly popular. If you have a pair that is heavy, you can purchase a strap that redistributes part of the weight to the shoulders and lower back.

Another valuable piece of equipment is a spotting scope. It is very useful when you are trying to sight waterfowl, shorebirds or soaring raptors, but it is really of no use if you are intent on seeing forest birds. A good spotting scope has a magnification of around 40x. It has a sturdy tripod or a window mount for the car. Be wary of second-hand models of telescopes, as they are designed for seeing stars, and their magnification is too great for birdwatching. One of the advantages of having a scope is that you will be able to see far-off birds, which can help during Seattle's winters (to see overwintering waterfowl and alcids) or during migration (to see shorebirds and raptors). By setting up in one spot (or by not even leaving your car) you can observe faraway flocks that would be little more than specks in your binoculars.

With these simple pieces of equipment (none of which is truly essential) and this handy field guide, anyone can enjoy birds in their area. Many birds are difficult to see because they stay hidden in treetops, but you can learn to identify them by their songs. After experiencing the thrill of a couple of hard-won identifications, you will find yourself taking your binoculars on walks, drives and trips to the beach and cabin. As rewards accumulate with experience, you may find the books and photos piling up and your trips being planned just to see birds!

BIRDING BY EAR

Sometimes, bird listening can be more effective than bird watching. The technique of birding by ear is gaining popularity, because listening for birds can be more efficient, productive and rewarding than waiting for a visual confirmation. Birds have distinctive songs that they use to resolve territorial disputes, and sound is therefore a useful way to identify species. It is particularly useful when trying to watch some of the smaller forest-dwelling birds. Their size and often indistinct plumage can make a visual search of the forest canopy frustrating. To facilitate auditory searches, catchy paraphrases are included in the descriptions of many of the birds. If the paraphrase just doesn't seem to work for you (they are often a personal thing) be creative and try to find one that fits. By spending time playing the song over in your head, fitting words to it, the voices of birds soon become as familiar as the voices of family members. Many excellent CDs and tapes are available at bookstores and wild-bird stores for the songs of the birds in your area.

KEEPING BIRD NOTES

Although most naturalists realize the usefulness of keeping accurate and concise notes of their observations, few are proud of their written records. It's easy to become overwhelmed by the excitement in the field and forget to jot down a few quick observations.

It's a good idea for every level of birdwatcher to get into the habit of carrying a soft, small notebook in a pocket or backpack. For the novice who is unsure of a bird's identity, a quick sketch (using a pencil is best), and a description of the bird's behavior and habits will help to confirm your sightings later. A simple line sketch is ideal, and it really doesn't matter how artistic it is! For more experienced birdwatchers, the activities of an observed bird and the dates on which it was seen can be accumulated over time as an ongoing personal study.

If you don't want to bother with a notebook, try a small, compact tape recorder to record field observations. The advantages to this method are its quickness and its usefulness in recording unfamiliar bird calls. By recording observations and calls, your field notes can be compiled at a later time in an unhurried manner.

A notebook provides an excellent way to remember and relive the moment in the field at a later time. A comprehensive notebook can even provide information to researchers who are looking at the dynamics of birds. Even keeping a count of feeder birds over a period of years can help ornithologists with their understanding of population ecology.

Another good way to learn about birds is to join your local Audubon or bird society. You will meet many knowledgeable people who will be glad to teach you what they know about birds, and to show you the best places to see them. Many organizations run field trips to some of the good birdwatching spots, and they provide the benefit of an expert to help with identification problems. Christmas Bird Counts are a highlight for birdwatchers, regardless of skill level. Look for information on these in your local paper.

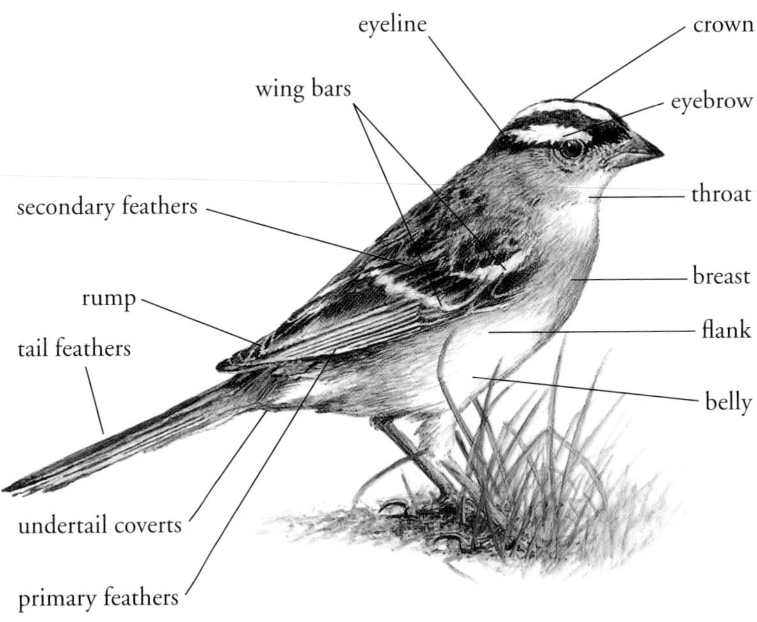

BIRDFEEDERS

They're messy, they can be costly, and they're sprouting up in neighborhoods everywhere. Feeding birds has become a common pastime in residential communities all over North America. Although the concept is fairly straightforward, as with anything else involving birds, feeders can become quite elaborate.

The great advantage to feeding birds is that neighborhood chickadees, jays, juncos and finches are enticed into regular visits. Don't expect birds to arrive at your feeder as soon as you set it up; it may take weeks for a few regulars to incorporate your yard into their daily routine. As the popularity of your feeder grows, the number of visiting birds will increase and more species will arrive. You will notice that your feeder is busier during the winter months, when natural foods are less abundant. You can increase the odds of a good avian turnout by using a variety of feeders and seeds. When a number of birds habitually visit your yard, maintaining the food source becomes a responsibility because they may have begun to rely on your feeder as a regular source of food.

Larger birds tend to enjoy feeding on platforms or on the ground, while smaller birds are comfortable on hanging seed dispensers. Certain seeds tend to attract specific birds; nature centres and wild-bird supply stores are the best places to ask how to attract a favorite species. It's mainly seed eaters that are attracted to backyards—some birds have no interest in feeders. Only the most committed birdwatcher will try to attract birds that are insect eaters, berry eaters, or, in some extreme cases, scavengers!

The location of the feeder may influence the amount of business it receives from the neighborhood birds. Because birds are wild, they are wary, and they are unlikely to visit an area where they may come under attack. When putting up your feeder, think like a bird. A good clear view with convenient escape routes is always appreciated. Cats like birdfeeders that are close to the ground and within pouncing distance from a bush; obviously, birds don't. Above all, a birdfeeder should be in view of a favorite window, where you can sit and enjoy the rewarding interaction of your appreciative feathered guests.

Glossary

accipiter: a forest hawk (genus *Accipiter*); characterized by a long tail and short, rounded wings; feeds mostly on birds.

alcid: a seabird of the auk family (Alcidae); includes auks, murres, puffins and guillemots.

brood: *n.* a family of young from one hatching; *v.* sit on eggs so as to hatch them.

coniferous: cone-producing trees, usually softwood evergreens (e.g., spruce, pine, fir).

corvid: a member of the crow family (Corvidae); includes crows, jays, magpies and ravens.

covey: a brood or flock of partridges, quail or grouse.

crop: an enlargement of the esophagus, serving as a storage structure and (in pigeons) has glands which produce secretions.

cryptic: coloration that blends with the environment.

dabbling: foraging technique used by ducks, where the head and neck are submerged but the body and tail remain on the water's surface.

dabbling duck: a duck that forages by dabbling; it can usually walk easily on land, it can take off without running, and it has a brightly coloured speculum; includes Mallards, Gadwalls, teals and others.

deciduous: a tree that loses its leaves annually (e.g., oak, maple, aspen, birch).

dimorphism: the existence of two distinct forms of a species, such as between the sexes.

eclipse: the dull, female-like plumage that male ducks breifly acquire after molting from their breeding plumage.

elbow patches: dark spots at the bend of the outstretched wing, seen from below.

flaking: a feeding behavior common to some woodpeckers, in which the bird breaks off flakes of bark from a tree to expose insects hidden underneath.

flycatching: feeding behavior where a bird leaves a perch, snatches an insect in mid-air, and returns to their previous perch; also known as 'hawking' or 'sallying.'

fledgling: a young chick that has just acquired its permanent flight feathers, but is still dependent on its parents.

flushing: a behavior where frightened birds explode into flight in response to a disturbance.

gape: the size of the mouth opening.

invertebrate: an animal that lacks a backbone or vertebral column (e.g., insects, spiders, molluks, worms).

irruption: a sporatic mass migration of birds into a non-breeding area.

larva: a development stage of an animal (usually an invertebrate) that has a different body form from the adult (e.g., caterpillar, maggot).

leading edge: the front edge of the wing as viewed from below.

litter: fallen plant material, such as twigs, leaves and needles, that forms a distinct layer above the soil, especially in forests.

lore: the small patch between the eye and the bill.

molting: the periodic replacement of worn out feathers (often twice a year).

morphology: the science of form and shape.

nape: the back of the neck.

neotropical migrant: a bird that nest in the Seattle area, but overwinters in the New World tropics.

niche: an ecological role filled by a species.

open country: a landscape that is primarily not forested.

parasitism: a relationship between two species where one benefits at the expense of the other.

phylogenetics: a method of classifying animals that puts the oldest ancestral groups before those that have arisen more recently.

pishing: making a sound to attract birds by saying *pishhh* as loudly and as wetly as comfortably possible.

polygynous: having a mating strategy where one male breeds with several females.

polyandrous: having a mating strategy where one female breeds with several males.

plucking post: a perch habitually used by an accipiter for plucking feathers from its prey.

raptor: a carnivorous (meat-eating) bird; includes eagles, hawks, falcons and owls.

rufous: rusty red in color.

speculum: a brightly colored patch in the wings of many dabbling ducks.

squeaking: making a sound to attract birds by loudly kissing the back of the hand, or by using a specially design squeaky bird call.

talons: the claws of birds of prey.

vertebrate: an animal that has a backbone or vertebral column (e.g., fish, amphibians, reptiles, birds, mammals).

understorey: the shrub or thicket layer beneath a canopy of trees.

References

American Ornithologists' Union. 1983. *Check-list of North American Birds.* 6th ed. American Ornithologists' Union, Washington, D.C.

American Ornithologists' Union. 1993. Thirty-ninth supplement to the American Ornithologists' Union *Check-list of North American Birds.* Auk 110:675–82.

American Ornithologists' Union. 1995. Fortieth supplement to the American Ornithologists' Union *Check-list of North American Birds.* Auk 112:819–30.

Ehrlich, P.R., D.S. Dobkin and D. Wheye. 1988. *The Birder's Handbook.* Fireside, New York.

Evans, H.E. 1993. *Pioneer Naturalists: The Discovery and Naming of North American Plants and Animals.* Henry Holt and Company, New York.

Farrand, J., ed. 1983. *The Audubon Society Master Guide to Birding.* Vols. 1–3. Alfred A. Knopf, New York.

Gabrielson, I.N., and S.G. Jewett. 1970. *Birds of the Pacific Northwest.* Dover, New York.

Gotch, A.F. 1981. *Birds: Their Latin Names Explained.* Blandford Press, Dorset, England.

Hunn, E.S. 1982. *Birding in Seattle and King County.* Seattle Audubon Society, Seattle.

Jewett, S.G. et al. 1953. *Birds of Washington State.* University of Washington Press, Seattle.

Larrison, E.J. 1981. *Birds of the Pacific Northwest.* University of Idaho Press, Moscow.

Lewis, M.G., and F.A. Sharpe. 1987. *Birding in the San Juan Islands.* The Mountaineers, Seattle.

MacRae, D. 1995. *Birder's Guide to Washington.* Gulf Publishing Company, Houston, Texas.

Mearns, B., and R. Mearns. 1992. *Audubon to Xantus: The Lives of Those Commemorated in North American Bird Names.* Academic Press, San Diego.

National Audubon Society. 1971–1995. *American Birds* Vols. 25–48.

Peterson, R.T. 1990. *A Field Guide to the Western Birds.* 3rd ed. Houghton Mifflin, Boston.

Book of North American Birds. The Reader's Digest Association Inc., Pleasantville, New York.

Robbins, C.S., B. Brunn, and H.S. Zim. 1966. *Birds of North America.* Golden Press, New York.

Scott. S.S. 1987. *Field Guide to the Birds of North America.* National Geographic Society, Washington, D.C.

Stokes, D., and L. Stokes. 1996. *Stokes Field Guide to Birds: Western Region.* Little, Brown and Co., Boston.

Terres, J.K. 1995. *The Audubon Society Encyclopedia of North American Birds.* Wings Books, New York.

Wahl, T.R., and D.R. Paulson. 1991. *A Guide to Bird Finding in Washington.* Rev. ed. T.R. Wahl, Bellingham, Washington.

Checklist of King County Birds

The following checklist is adapted from the Seattle Audubon Society's *Birding in Seattle and King County* (Hunn 1982). This list may be used to record the species you have seen in King County. Subspecies are indented; introduced species carry an asterisk (*); species considered 'accidental' in King County are italicized; bird families are separated by an extra space.

The letter codes that follow the species names describe breeding status and peak abundance:

- N One or more confirmed nesting records for the county.
- N? A species presumed to breed in the county, but for which no definite nesting occurrence has been recorded.
- Ne A species that formerly bred in the county, but has not done so for the past 30 years (an extirpated nester).
- X A species recorded five or fewer times in the county.
- r Rare: Careful search and a measure of luck are required, even in appropriate habitat at the peak season.
- u Uncommon: Regularly found in appropriate habitat at the peak season, but only in small numbers; may be missed if not specifically searched for.
- c Common: Seen on most field trips to appropriate habitat at the peak season.

- ❑ Red-throated Loon .... u
- ❑ Arctic Loon .... r
- ❑ Common Loon .... N?, u
- ❑ *Yellow-billed Loon* X

- ❑ Pied-billed Grebe .... N, c
- ❑ Horned Grebe c
- ❑ Red-necked Grebe c
- ❑ Eared Grebe .... r
- ❑ Western Grebe c
- ❑ *Clark's Grebe* X

- ❑ *Northern Fulmar* X
- ❑ *Sooty Shearwater* X
- ❑ *Short-tailed Shearwater* X

- ❑ *American White Pelican* X

- ❑ Double-crested Cormorant c
- ❑ Brandt's Cormorant .... r
- ❑ Pelagic Cormorant .... u

- ❑ American Bittern .... N?, r
- ❑ Great Blue Heron .... N, c
- ❑ *Great Egret* X
- ❑ *Cattle Egret* X
- ❑ Green Heron .... N, u
- ❑ Black-crowned Night-Heron .... r
- ❑ Tundra Swan .... r
- ❑ Trumpeter Swan .... r
- ❑ Greater White-fronted Goose .... r
- ❑ Snow Goose .... r
- ❑ *Emperor Goose* X
- ❑ Brant c
- ❑ Canada Goose* .... N, c
  - ❑ Cackling Goose .... r
  - ❑ *Aleutian Canada Goose* X
  - ❑ Lesser Canada Goose c
  - ❑ Dusky Canada Goose X
- ❑ Wood Duck .... N, r
- ❑ Green-winged Teal .... N, c
- ❑ Eurasian Teal .... r
- ❑ American Black Duck* .... r
- ❑ Mallard .... N, c
- ❑ Northern Pintail .... N, c
- ❑ Blue-winged Teal .... N, u
- ❑ Cinnamon Teal .... N, u
- ❑ Northern Shoveler .... N, c
- ❑ Gadwall .... N, u
- ❑ Eurasian Wigeon .... r
- ❑ American Wigeon .... N?, c
- ❑ Canvasback .... N?, u
- ❑ Redhead .... r
- ❑ Ring-necked Duck .... N?, u
- ❑ *Tufted Duck* X
- ❑ Greater Scaup c

- ❑ Lesser Scaup .... N, c
- ❑ *King Eider* X
- ❑ Harlequin Duck .... N, u
- ❑ Oldsquaw .... r
- ❑ Black Scoter .... u
- ❑ Surf Scoter c
- ❑ White-winged Scoter c
- ❑ Common Goldeneye c
- ❑ Barrow's Goldeneye .... N?, u
- ❑ Bufflehead c
- ❑ Hooded Merganser .... N, u
- ❑ Common Merganser .... N, c
- ❑ Red-breasted Merganser c
- ❑ Ruddy Duck .... N, c

- ❑ Turkey Vulture .... u

- ❑ Osprey .... N, u
- ❑ Bald Eagle .... N, u
- ❑ Northern Harrier .... N?, u
- ❑ Sharp-shinned Hawk .... N?, u
- ❑ Cooper's Hawk .... N, u
- ❑ Northern Goshawk .... N, r
- ❑ *Swainson's Hawk* X
- ❑ Red-tailed Hawk .... N, c
- ❑ *Harlan's Hawk* X
- ❑ Rough-legged Hawk .... r
- ❑ Golden Eagle .... N, r

- ❑ American Kestrel .... N, u
- ❑ Merlin .... N, u
- ❑ Peregrine Falcon .... r
- ❑ Gyrfalcon .... r

- ❑ Ring-necked Pheasant* .... N, c
- ❑ Spruce Grouse .... N?, r
- ❑ Blue Grouse .... N, u
- ❑ White-tailed Ptarmigan .... N, r
- ❑ Ruffed Grouse .... N, u
- ❑ Northern Bobwhite* .... Ne
- ❑ California Quail* .... N, c
- ❑ Mountain Quail .... Ne

- ❑ Virginia Rail .... N, u
- ❑ Sora .... N, u
- ❑ American Coot .... N, c

- ❑ *Sandhill Crane* X

- ❑ Black-bellied Plover .... r
- ❑ American Golden-Plover .... r
- ❑ Semipalmated Plover .... u
- ❑ Killdeer .... N, c

- ❑ *Black Oystercatcher* X

- ❑ *American Avocet* X

- ❑ Greater Yellowlegs .... u
- ❑ Lesser Yellowlegs .... u
- ❑ Solitary Sandpiper .... r
- ❑ *Willet* X
- ❑ Wandering Tattler .... r
- ❑ Spotted Sandpiper .... N, u
- ❑ Whimbrel .... r
- ❑ *Long-billed Curlew* X
- ❑ *Marbled Godwit* X
- ❑ *Black Turnstone* X
- ❑ *Surfbird* X
- ❑ Sanderling .... u
- ❑ Semipalmated Sandpiper .... r
- ❑ Western Sandpiper .... u
- ❑ Least Sandpiper .... u
- ❑ Baird's Sandpiper .... r
- ❑ Pectoral Sandpiper .... u
- ❑ Dunlin .... u
- ❑ *Stilt Sandpiper* X
- ❑ *Buff-breasted Sandpiper* X
- ❑ Short-billed Dowitcher .... r
- ❑ Long-billed Dowitcher .... u
- ❑ Common Snipe .... N, u
- ❑ Wilson's Phalarope .... r
- ❑ Red-necked Phalarope .... r

- ❑ *Pomarine Jaeger* X
- ❑ Parasitic Jaeger .... u
- ❑ *Long-tailed Jaeger* X
- ❑ Franklin's Gull .... r
- ❑ Little Gull .... r
- ❑ Bonaparte's Gull c
- ❑ Heermann's Gull .... u
- ❑ Mew Gull c
- ❑ Ring-billed Gull .... u
- ❑ California Gull c
- ❑ Herring Gull .... u
- ❑ Thayer's Gull .... u
- ❑ Western Gull .... r
- ❑ Glaucous-winged Gull .... N, c
- ❑ *Glaucous Gull* X
- ❑ Black-legged Kittiwake .... r
- ❑ *Sabine's Gull* X
- ❑ Caspian Tern .... r
- ❑ Common Tern c
- ❑ *Arctic Tern* X
- ❑ *Forster's Tern* X
- ❑ Black Tern .... r

- ❑ Common Murre .... u
- ❑ Pigeon Guillemot .... N, u
- ❑ Marbled Murrelet .... N?, u
- ❑ Ancient Murrelet .... u
- ❑ *Cassin's Auklet* X
- ❑ Rhinoceros Auklet c
- ❑ *Tufted Puffin* X

❑ Rock Dove* .... N, c
❑ Band-tailed Pigeon .... N, c
❑ Mourning Dove .... N?, r

❑ *Yellow-billed Cuckoo* .... Ne, X

❑ Barn Owl .... N, c

❑ *Flammulated Owl* X
❑ Western Screech-Owl .... N, c
❑ Great Horned Owl .... N, c
❑ Snowy Owl .... u
❑ Northern Pygmy-Owl .... N, u
❑ Burrowing Owl X
❑ Spotted Owl .... N, r
❑ Barred Owl .... N, r
❑ *Great Gray Owl* X
❑ *Long-eared Owl* X
❑ Short-eared Owl .... N, u
❑ Northern Saw-whet Owl .... N, u

❑ Common Nighthawk .... N, u
❑ *Common Poor-will* X

❑ Black Swift .... N?, u
❑ Vaux's Swift .... N, c

❑ Anna's Hummingbird .... N, r
❑ Rufous Hummingbird .... N, c
❑ *Allen's Hummingbird* X

❑ Belted Kingfisher .... N, u

❑ Lewis's Woodpecker .... Ne, r
❑ Yellow-bellied Sapsucker .... N?, r
❑ Red-breasted Sapsucker .... N, c
❑ *Williamson's Sapsucker* X
❑ Downy Woodpecker .... N, c
❑ Hairy Woodpecker .... N, u
❑ *Three-toed Woodpecker* X
❑ *Black-backed Woodpecker* X
Northern Flicker ....
❑ Red-shafted Flicker .... N, c
❑ Yellow-shafted Flicker .... r
❑ Pileated Woodpecker .... N, u

❑ Olive-sided Flycatcher .... N, c
❑ Western Wood-Pewee .... N, c
❑ Willow Flycatcher .... N, c
❑ Hammond's Flycatcher .... N, u
❑ *Dusky Flycatcher* X
❑ Pacific-slope Flycatcher .... N, c
❑ Say's Phoebe .... r
❑ *Ash-throated Flycatcher* X
❑ Western Kingbird .... r
❑ Eastern Kingbird .... N, r

❑ Horned Lark .... r

❑ Purple Martin .... N, r
❑ Tree Swallow .... N, u
❑ Violet-green Swallow .... N, c
❑ Northern Rough-winged Swallow .... N, u
❑ Bank Swallow X
❑ Cliff Swallow .... N, c
❑ Barn Swallow .... N, c

❑ Gray Jay .... N, c
❑ Steller's Jay .... N, c
❑ *Blue Jay* X
❑ *Western Scrub-Jay* X
❑ *Clark's Nutcracker* X
❑ Black-billed Magpie .... r
❑ American Crow .... N, c
❑ Northwestern Crow .... N, u
❑ Common Raven .... N, u

❑ Black-capped Chickadee .... N, c
❑ Mountain Chickadee .... N?, r
❑ Chestnut-backed Chickadee .... N, c

❑ Bushtit .... N, c

❑ Red-breasted Nuthatch .... N, u
❑ White-breasted Nuthatch X

❑ Brown Creeper .... N, u

❑ *Rock Wren* X
❑ Bewick's Wren .... N, c
❑ House Wren .... N?, r
❑ Winter Wren .... N, c
❑ Marsh Wren .... N, c

❑ American Dipper .... N, u

❑ Golden-crowned Kinglet .... N, c
❑ Ruby-crowned Kinglet c
❑ Western Bluebird .... Ne, r
❑ Mountain Bluebird .... N?, r
❑ Townsend's Solitaire .... N, u
❑ *Veery* X
❑ Swainson's Thrush .... N, c
❑ Hermit Thrush .... N, c
❑ American Robin .... N, c
❑ Varied Thrush .... N, u

❑ *Gray Catbird* X
❑ Northern Mockingbird .... r
❑ *Sage Thrasher* X
❑ *Brown Thrasher* X

- ❑ *White Wagtail* X
- ❑ American Pipit .... N, c

- ❑ Bohemian Waxwing .... u
- ❑ Cedar Waxwing .... N, c

- ❑ Northern Shrike .... u
- ❑ *Loggerhead Shrike* X

- ❑ European Starling* .... N, c

- ❑ *White-eyed Vireo* X
- ❑ Solitary Vireo .... N, u
- ❑ Hutton's Vireo .... N, u
- ❑ Warbling Vireo .... N, c
- ❑ Red-eyed Vireo .... N, u

- ❑ *Tennessee Warbler* X
- ❑ Orange-crowned Warbler .... N, c
- ❑ Nashville Warbler .... N?, r
- ❑ Yellow Warbler .... N, c
- Yellow-rumped Warbler
  - ❑ Audubon's Warbler .... N, c
  - ❑ Myrtle Warbler .... u
- ❑ Black-throated Gray Warbler .... N, c
- ❑ Townsend's Warbler .... N, c
- ❑ Hermit Warbler .... N?, r
- ❑ *Palm Warbler* X
- ❑ *Black-and-white Warbler* X
- ❑ *Ovenbird* X
- ❑ *Northern Waterthrush* X
- ❑ MacGillivray's Warbler .... N, u
- ❑ Common Yellowthroat .... N, c
- ❑ *Hooded Warbler* X
- ❑ Wilson's Warbler .... N, c
- ❑ Yellow-breasted Chat .... Ne, r
- ❑ Western Tanager .... N, c
- ❑ *Rose-breasted Grosbeak* X
- ❑ Black-headed Grosbeak .... N, u
- ❑ Lazuli Bunting .... N?, r
- ❑ *Green-tailed Towhee* X
- ❑ Spotted Towhee .... N, c
- ❑ American Tree Sparrow .... r
- ❑ Chipping Sparrow .... N, r
- ❑ Vesper Sparrow .... N?, r
- ❑ *Lark Sparrow* X
- ❑ *Black-throated Sparrow* X
- ❑ *Sage Sparrow* X
- ❑ Savannah Sparrow .... N, c
- ❑ Fox Sparrow .... N, c
- ❑ Song Sparrow .... N, c
- ❑ Lincoln's Sparrow .... N, u
- ❑ *Swamp Sparrow* X
- ❑ White-throated Sparrow .... r
- ❑ Golden-crowned Sparrow c
- ❑ White-crowned Sparrow .... N, c
- ❑ Harris' Sparrow .... r
- Dark-eyed Junco
  - ❑ Oregon Junco .... N, c
  - ❑ Slate-colored Junco .... r
- ❑ Lapland Longspur .... r
- ❑ Snow Bunting .... r
- ❑ *Bobolink* X
- ❑ Red-winged Blackbird .... N, c
- ❑ Western Meadowlark .... N, u
- ❑ Yellow-headed Blackbird .... r
- ❑ Brewer's Blackbird .... N, c
- ❑ Common Grackle X
- ❑ Brown-headed Cowbird .... N, c
- ❑ Bullock's Oriole .... N, u

- ❑ *Brambling* X
- ❑ Gray-crowned Rosy-Finch .... N, r
- ❑ Pine Grosbeak .... r
- ❑ Purple Finch .... N, u
- ❑ *Cassin's Finch* X
- ❑ House Finch .... N, c
- ❑ Red Crossbill .... N, c
- ❑ *White-winged Crossbill* X
- ❑ Common Redpoll .... r
- ❑ Pine Siskin .... N, c
- ❑ American Goldfinch .... N, c
- ❑ Evening Grosbeak .... N, c

- ❑ House Sparrow* .... N, c

Index of Common Names

Boldface page numbers refer to primary, illustrated entries.

Index of Scientific Names

This index only references the primary species treatments.

About the Author

When he's not out watching birds, frogs or snakes, Chris Fisher researches endangered species management and wildlife interpretation in the Department of Renewable Resources at the University of Alberta. The appeal of western wildlife and wilderness has led to many travels, including frequent visits with the birds of the Pacific coast. By sharing his enthusiasm and passion for wild things through lectures, photographs and articles, Chris strives to foster a greater appreciation for the value of our wilderness.